# In Case of War

# In Case of War

*Seth Laurengas*

∞

1st Edition / 1st Print 2024
Piamo Press
www.piamo.no

Graphic Design and Cover: Pia Haugseth
Editor: Hide Text Services AS / Kristin Hide

Set in Adobe Garamond Pro and Gill Sans

All inquiries regarding rights should be directed to:
pia@piamo.dev

# CONTENTS

Throughout the years, I have traveled the world, for various reasons and with different purposes. Along the way, I have witnessed the extremes of humanity—its greatness as well as its darkest sides. Many times, I lost faith that we as people could unite for the good of all, but a person I met recently changed that for me.

With renewed hope, and perhaps a hint of optimism, I now wish to share the knowledge I've gathered in war and crisis situations. My hope is that my contribution can be decisive for those going through their own dark times, helping them emerge victorious—both physically and mentally.

I do not claim to have all the answers, but perhaps—just perhaps—my experience can help one person in need. I therefore dedicate this book to humanity, in the hope that we may one day find our way to a better version of ourselves.

—Seth

# PREFACE

The idea to create a small survival book for families in case of war or crisis came from a woman with such concern for her fellow human beings that I simply could not resist writing it. She is unique, and a rarity in world society in terms of the love she has for her fellow human beings. She is a light in the darkness.

The book is intended to provide advice and understanding for difficult choices that must be made when it comes to moral and ethical principles, and help and explanations for self-help to survive in a war or crisis situation.

The book itself is not mandatory or indicative, just advisory in the simplest sense. It cannot guarantee survival either, but will go a long way in helping you to be able to overcome critical situations, should they arise.

Each country has its own laws and regulations that citizens must take into account, and it is important that you follow the national guidelines in case of a crisis.

# INTRODUCTION

In a world where uncertainty and crisis situations can arise without warning, it is more important than ever to be prepared. I have built up my experience and knowledge through many years of experience in crisis management around the world in the private sector. I have felt on my body what it is like to be in extreme crises.

As the world around us collapses, we are all faced with impossible choices. In such situations, when help is far away, we must rely on our own strength and knowledge. But what do you do if you don't have the necessary experience? This book is here to fill that void. It gives you practical tools and insight into how you can protect yourself, your family, your pets, your fellow humans and your local community - both in the immediate crisis and in the time afterwards.

Over the years, I have learned that cooperation and community are essential for survival. Understanding the importance of human support, empathy and unity can make the difference between chaos and order. I will share how to build and maintain strong, supportive relationships in extreme situations, as well as how to help others without putting yourself in unnecessary danger.

Effective strategies for survival include both physical and mental preparation. From building an emergency kit to learning basic first aid, I'll cover the essentials you need to know. Planning for evacuation, finding safe places and ensuring access to food, water and medicine are factors I have experienced as vitally important.

War and crisis situations can put our moral and ethical boundaries to the test. How does one balance the need for one's own survival with the need for, or the duty to, help others? What do you do when faced with impossible choices? Through examples and reflections from my own experiences, I will discuss these difficult questions and provide you with guidance to navigate them in a way that maintains our humanity.

Having knowledge and skills in place before a crisis occurs can save lives. This book is not only a guide for extreme situations, but also a tool for building resilience and preparedness in everyday life. By being prepared, we can reduce fear and increase our ability to act quickly and effectively when it really matters.

Our loved ones are often the ones we are most worried about in a crisis. How can we ensure that children feel safe and protected? What are the best ways to include family pets in emergency plans? I will provide advice and strategies to care for the whole family, including the four-legged members.

Knowledge of the laws and regulations that apply during crises is necessary to navigate correctly. This includes everything from evacuation procedures to rights and duties in conflict zones. I will cover the basic legal aspects you should be aware of in order to get the best possible out of various situations.

Finally, I will go through how a society can be rebuilt after a crisis, both on an individual and societal level.

This book is your companion in an uncertain world, a guide to keeping your head cool, your heart warm and your loved ones safe.

# PREPARATION FOR WAR AND CRISES

Let's begin this journey together, towards a world where we stand stronger in the face of crises.

When we think of war or severe crises, it often seems distant—something that happens elsewhere. But in an increasingly unpredictable world, being prepared is more important than ever. Preparation isn't just about gathering supplies; it's about understanding risks, creating a plan, and knowing how to respond when disaster strikes. In this chapter, I'll outline how you can best prepare yourself and your loved ones.

When I speak about the importance of planning before a crisis like war, I'm especially thinking of you as a civilian. Through my years in the field, I have seen how good planning can mean the difference between life and death. When a crisis hits, chaos and panic are often the first reactions. But if you and your family have a plan, you know what to do, and you can stay calm. That can save lives.

A solid plan ensures that you know where to go and how to get there. You need clear evacuation instructions so that you can reach safety as quickly as possible. This means knowing where the shelters are and making sure they are well-stocked with essentials like food, water, and medicine. It's also important to have plans for maintaining essential services such as healthcare, water supply, and communication. This ensures that, even in chaos, you have access to the basics you need to survive.

Cooperation is key in such situations. Plan with neighbors, family, and your community. Make agreements about how you can help each other, and establish clear lines of communication. This way, you can coordinate efforts and support one another when it's needed most.

Training and drills are also essential. Make it a habit to review your plans regularly, and conduct drills so everyone knows what to do. This is especially important for children and the elderly, who may need extra help. Then, when the time comes, it will be easier to act quickly and correctly.

When a crisis hits, having a plan helps you make better decisions. It provides a framework to follow, reducing stress and enabling you to act more rationally. Additionally, it gives you a sense of security.

Overall, advance planning offers a structured approach to crisis management. I have seen firsthand how this works; a good plan can make the difference between survival and failure. It is also crucial for minimizing damage and ensuring that you can return to a normal daily life as quickly as possible.

**Risk Assessment and Planning**

There's a difference between how defense forces and civilians conduct risk analysis. Understanding and identifying potential hazards can be a bit challenging, but imagine creating a mental overview of your area.

Assess the likelihood of risks arising. In the context of war and crises, this might mean evaluating geographic, political, and social factors that could impact your community. For example, do you live near a politically unstable region or in an area prone to natural disasters? Understand which threats are most relevant to you so you can plan accordingly.

**Next step: Make a plan.**

Having a plan equips you and your family with strategies for how to respond to different scenarios, such as evacuation or sheltering in place. Start by gathering family members or those you want involved. It's important that everyone participates and understands what needs to be done. Include details such as who is responsible for what, where to meet, and what to bring. A good plan is simple, clear, and known to everyone involved.

## Emergency Supplies

What do you really need? When a crisis strikes, getting necessary supplies may be difficult, so it's essential to stock up on key items in advance. This includes food, water, medicines, hygiene products, and essential documents. Note that storing these items requires careful consideration of shelf life, storage space, and accessibility. For example, choose foods with a long shelf life, that require minimal preparation, and that provide adequate nutrition. Look at your dietary habits: how would you build an ideal stockpile for your preferences? There is care in food and in preparing a good meal. It helps if meals can be prepared quickly and with minimal equipment. Remember that you may not have any equipment if you're forced to flee.

If you have to leave everything behind, what will you take with you? Clothes, in general, are heavy to carry, and you may have to carry everything yourself. If you have small children or pets, you may need to carry them as well. The more you can plan, the better. And set vanity aside. If a crisis strikes, it's important to conserve energy and prioritize so that you and your loved ones can reach safety quickly.

## The Most Important First: Water

Water is the most critical resource in a crisis. You should store at least 3 liters of water per person per day, for both drinking and hygiene. Use sturdy, opaque containers that seal tightly, and store them in a cool, dark place to prevent bacterial growth. Look around: is there somewhere you can collect water from natural sources? That could be useful for cleaning. Also, learn how to purify water from natural sources through boiling, filtration, or chemical purification tablets.

Your emergency supply kit should include the following, for both sheltering at home and rapid evacuation:

## Food and Water

- At least 3 liters of water per person per day for a minimum of 7 days (bottled water or containers). Store in a dark, cool place.
- Non-perishable food for at least 7 days per person (canned goods, dry food, energy bars).
- Manual can opener, cutlery, plates, cups.

## Medications and First Aid

- Personal medications for at least 7 days. Painkillers, allergy medication, and other over-the-counter medications.
- Iodine tablets (for radiation exposure or risk of exposure).
- First aid supplies: Bandages, antiseptics, scissors, tweezers, thermometer.

## Emergency Equipment

- LED flashlight with extra rechargeable batteries.
- Battery-powered or hand-crank radio to receive news and alerts.
- Extra rechargeable batteries for other devices.
- Battery or solar charger for various types of batteries.
- Whistle and emergency flare for signaling help.
- Matches or stormproof lighter with lighter fluid. Store in a waterproof container.
- Emergency charger for mobile phone: solar or battery-powered.
- Communication equipment: Walkie-talkie (preferably with long range and multi-channel).
- Tools: Hammer, knife, saw, screwdrivers, nails, and other essentials.
- Rope/climbing rope, various carabiners, and climbing harness.

## Hygiene Items

- Toilet paper, soap, toothbrush, toothpaste.
- Wet wipes, antiseptic wipes, hand sanitizer.
- Sanitary products: Pads, tampons, nail clippers, scissors.

- Diapers and baby care products (if needed).

**Clothing and Blankets**
- Warm clothes (wool), rain gear, and comfortable shoes.
- Outdoor clothing such as windproof jacket and pants.
- Wool blankets or sleeping bags for warmth and comfort.

**Documents and Cash**

- Important documents: Copies of ID, passport, insurance papers, bank information, medical records.
- Cash: Small bills and coins in case banks are unavailable; ideally, have at least two different currencies.

**Miscellaneous**

- Multi-tool or pocket knife.
- Map of the area for navigation without GPS.
- Compass: Learn how to use it with the map.
- Notebook and pens.
- Personal items: Glasses, contact lenses and accessories, hearing aids and batteries, etc.

## FOR EVACUETING

- A sturdy, lightweight backpack. Waterproof cover or bag, foldable ground mat, compression sleeping bag.
- One set of extra clothes and underwear per person (light wool layers and wind- and waterproof outerwear).
- Water: At least one bottle per person and water purification tablets (hydration pack optional).
- Food: Energy or granola bars, nuts, dried fruit (non-perishable food with long shelf life in all conditions).
- Medications: Enough for at least one week, including prescription medications (ideally with copies of prescriptions, if available).
- Iodine tablets.
- Basic first aid kit: Compact essentials.
- Emergency Gear: Strong LED flashlight, spare batteries, whistle, emergency flare or rocket, multi-tool knife, matches,

stormproof lighter, gas refill for lighter, fire starters, small foldable axe/shovel, hunting knife, emergency blanket.
- Hygiene Items: Toothbrush, toothpaste, antiseptic wipes, compact travel towel for each person (quick-drying).
- Documents: Copies of important papers in a waterproof container (passport, driver's license, national ID, bank cards, birth certificates, donor card, health card, insurance papers, other relevant licenses, and certificates).
- Cash: At least two different currencies. Small bills and coins (cash amount should not exceed what you can afford to lose).
- Mobile Phone and Emergency Charger
- Solar or kinetic charger, walkie-talkie with extra-long antennas to increase communication range (long-distance).

**For Special Needs**

**Children:** Diapers, milk, baby food, toys, blankets.
**Elderly:** Extra medication, aids.
**Pets:** Food, water, carrier, necessary medications.

This emergency kit is designed to support survival both at home and during rapid evacuation. Store it in an easily accessible location, and regularly check to update and replace expired food and medications. Practice packing the emergency bag and conduct evacuation drills regularly.

## MENTAL PREPAREDNESS

### Why Mental Strength is Important

While physical preparations are essential, mental preparedness is equally vital. In a crisis, it's natural to feel scared or overwhelmed, but those who have prepared mentally are more likely to stay calm and act effectively. When people are stressed, it's easy to make poor decisions, so learning techniques to manage stress can be highly beneficial. Techniques like breathing exercises, visualizing solutions, and learning to stay calm can help you handle challenging situations. Panicking can make things worse. Having mental strength is more important than physical endurance in the initial stages. You can build physical fitness along the way, but being mentally prepared will make a big difference if something happens.

To strengthen your mental resilience, start by practicing various scenarios in your mind. Visualize how you would respond in an emergency, and go over your plans repeatedly until they feel natural. Remember that military training regularly involves rehearsing how to handle different situations; the more they repeat, the more automatic their actions become when needed. Involve the whole family in these exercises, especially children. Keep in mind that mental strength also involves being flexible and adapting when things don't go as planned, which can be crucial for survival. Showing care and fostering a sense of mastery in those around you will strengthen your team when it truly matters.

## IMPROVING MENTAL STRENGTH AND RESILIENCE

### Stress Management

Mindfulness and Meditation: Practicing mindfulness and meditation regularly can help you develop the ability to focus and calm your mind under stress. It can enhance your capacity to manage panic and make rational decisions during critical moments.

Visualization: Practice visualizing different crisis scenarios and how you would respond. This can mentally prepare you for what might happen, making you more aware of the actions you may need to take.

## PHYSICAL PREPARATION

In a world filled with uncertainty, where natural disasters, economic collapse, and armed conflicts can occur without warning, it is more important than ever for civilians to be physically prepared. Physical preparation isn't just about being able to run fast or lift heavy objects; it's about developing a body that can withstand the physical challenges that may arise in a crisis or war situation.

## Building Physical Endurance

Physical endurance is the foundation of survival in any crisis. Endurance gives you the capacity to move long distances, carry heavy loads, and continue functioning effectively despite fatigue.

### Cardio Training

**Running and Walking:** Regular running, brisk walking, or hiking strengthens your heart and lung capacity. Start with short distances, and gradually increase the length and intensity of your sessions. This will enable you to evacuate quickly, carry equipment, or move through rough terrain if necessary.

**Cycling:** Cycling is another effective way to improve endurance while strengthening your leg muscles. It can also serve as an alternative means of transportation during a crisis if motorized vehicles are unavailable.

### Strength Training

**Bodyweight Exercises:** Push-ups, pull-ups, squats, and planks are examples of exercises that can be done without equipment and strengthen key muscle groups. These are crucial when you need to lift, carry, or climb in a crisis situation.

**Weight Training:** If you have access to weights, include exercises such as deadlifts, shoulder presses, and rows in your training program. These exercises strengthen your core muscles and prepare you for handling physical stress, such as lifting heavy objects or enduring long periods of activity under pressure.

### Flexibility and Mobility

**Stretching:** Daily stretching routines improve your flexibility, reducing the risk of injury when performing unusual movements like crawling, climbing, or jumping over obstacles.

**Yoga and Pilates:** These activities not only help with flexibility but also with balance and body control, which are essential in stressful situations.

## EVACUATION AND SURVIVAL IN URBAN AREAS

In a crisis, you may be forced to leave your home or community. Being physically prepared for a quick evacuation can mean the difference between life and death.

### Packing an Emergency Bag

A good emergency bag should contain everything you need to survive the first 72 hours. This includes food, water, clothing, first aid supplies, tools, and protective gear. The training mentioned earlier should include regular exercises involving carrying the bag to build strength and endurance, as well as to test the weight distribution and comfort of the pack.

### Navigation Without GPS

In case GPS systems or phone networks stop working, you must be able to navigate without tools. Practice using maps and compasses, and also follow the sun's position or the stars at night.

### Self-Defense and Conflict Management

Learn basic self-defense techniques to protect yourself and your loved ones from potential threats. At the same time, it's important to understand how to de-escalate dangerous situations. The ability to stay calm and make rational decisions can be just as important as physical strength in a threatening situation.


## MAINTAINING HEALTH IN CRISIS SITUATIONS

### First Aid Knowledge

Attend a first aid course to learn how to treat common injuries such as cuts, fractures, or burns. Knowledge of CPR (Cardiopulmonary Resuscitation) can save lives in an emergency situation.

### Hygiene and Disease Prevention

In a crisis, diseases can spread quickly due to poor hygiene. Make sure to maintain good hand hygiene and have access to disinfectants. Avoid consuming food or water that may be contaminated.

## Nutrition and Immune System

Eat a balanced diet that strengthens your immune system. During times of crisis, it may be necessary to supplement with vitamins and minerals, especially vitamin C, D, and zinc, all of which support immune health.

# CHAPTER 2

# SAFETY AND PROTECTION

When a crisis occurs, safety is your highest priority. This includes both physical safety—avoiding direct harm from threats such as acts of war, natural disasters, or violence—and the protection of your resources and assets. Knowing how to protect yourself, your family, and your home can be essential for survival in chaotic situations. In this chapter, I describe practical methods for achieving this.

## Why Securing Your Home is Important

Your home can serve as your base during a crisis. It's the place where you store supplies, protect your family, and may take shelter for extended periods. However, for your home to function as a safe haven, it must be secure against intruders and other dangers. Understanding the importance of security can help protect you in extremely stressful conditions. Based on many years of experience, I provide a thorough overview of the significance of securing your home in such situations, with concrete examples of how to proceed.

## Protection Against Physical Harm

During war or crises, there is a significant risk of physical harm from direct attacks or incidental explosions. By reinforcing the structure of your building, sealing holes or cracks, and building protective barriers, you'll be in a safer environment. During World War II, many buildings in Britain were reinforced with sandbags and concrete plates to protect against air raids, helping to reduce injuries and save lives.

## Security and Psychological Stability

A secured home will give you a greater sense of safety and stability when the outside world is chaotic. Creating a mental refuge at home during prolonged crises can help you emerge mentally stronger. During the conflict in Syria, it became common for families to build safe rooms at home, not only for physical safety but also to maintain a sense of normalcy and security. In some cases, complex safe rooms with secret exits were built, almost like a fully equipped home within a home. This depends on your resources, of course, but creating a safe space can make a big difference.

## Preventing Break-ins and Theft

When social structures break down, crime rates can quickly rise. Practically any home can become a target for theft, looting, or occupation. Securing your home can prevent break-ins, protect valuable assets, and ward off unwanted visitors. During the economic crisis in Venezuela, many homes were secured with extra locks, grilles, and alarm systems to prevent break-ins due to increased poverty and social unrest.

## Access Control

In crisis situations, it may be crucial to control who has access to your home. This can prevent unauthorized entry from strangers or potentially dangerous individuals. During the conflict in Ukraine, many families have used security systems like surveillance cameras and access control. When war breaks out, there's an immediate increase in pressure on emergency services, which can easily be exploited by criminal groups, enemies, and trespassers. Social rules can vanish, turning everyday life from safe to insecure.

## Preparedness for Emergencies

A secured home offers better opportunities to handle emergencies such as fires, floods, or other unforeseen events. During Hurricane Katrina in the USA, homes that had been secured with solid structural improvements and emergency systems were better able to handle flooding and destruction.

### Storage of Reserves

In crisis situations, it's crucial to have stored essential resources such as food, water, medicines, and other supplies. A secured home provides a safe place for these stores. During the Cuban Missile Crisis in 1962, many households set up secure storage areas for food and other essentials as part of their emergency plans. Households with secured storage spaces coped better during the crisis than those who had not implemented such security measures.

### Managing Personal Resources

Securing your home is not only about physical protection but also about maintaining mental stability, managing resources, and controlling access. A well-secured home can be a lifesaving advantage in times of uncertainty and danger. By implementing effective security measures, you can better protect yourself, your loved ones, and your valuable assets, such as documents and other irreplaceable items. During the ethnic conflicts in Rwanda in the 1990s, many families took steps to hide and secure important documents and possessions to protect against looting and loss.

## STRATEGIES FOR SECURING YOUR HOME

**To secure your home, consider the following strategies:**

- **Physical Reinforcements:** Install security doors and window grilles, and use equipment that can withstand attacks or break-ins.

- **Surveillance Systems:** Use cameras and alarm systems to monitor and alert you to any suspicious activity.

- **Storage:** Organize the storage of essential supplies in a secure location that is easy to access.

- **Escape Routes:** Have planned escape routes and secure locations to protect yourself and your loved ones if you need to evacuate.

**Fire and Gas Leak Prevention**

During crises, infrastructure may be damaged, increasing the risk of fires or gas leaks. Ensure you have functioning smoke detectors and fire extinguishers, as well as a plan for rapid evacuation in case of fire. Gas lines should be shut off if there is a risk of leaks, and everyone in the household should know how to do this. Once again, it's beneficial to conduct fire and gas leak drills at home so everyone is aware of what to do if a crisis arises.

## ANIMALS AND PETS IN A CRISIS

If you have animals, you may quickly face difficult decisions, and it's essential to create an emergency plan for them as well. Starting with livestock, find safe locations nearby where the animals can stay. Open pastures might be less exposed than buildings. Ensure you have an evacuation plan with appropriate transportation if circumstances make it urgent to move the animals. Stock up on enough food and water for several weeks, and be aware that in an extreme situation, you might have to leave the animals behind. Make sure they are registered so they can be tracked if they get separated from you. It can be advantageous to connect with neighbors and nearby farms so you can cooperate to protect the animals. Additionally, have a plan for humane euthanasia if the situation becomes critical enough to prevent suffering. Being prepared in these ways increases the chances of livestock surviving conflicts.

For pets, evaluate how best to protect and care for them. If you have a dog, consider whether it might serve a useful role in a crisis, such as alerting you to dangers or providing comfort. Practicing staying in a crate can help reduce stress for your furry friend. Ensure you have an emergency kit ready with essentials like first aid supplies, food, water, favorite toys, blankets, and necessary medications. An ID tag with your contact information can help in reuniting you if you get separated. Practice evacuating with your pet, as you may face a situation where it's critical to get everyone out, including your pet. Have you prepared a temporary shelter for your pet or identified a pet-friendly refuge? These are things to plan in advance.

No matter what pet you have, it can play an important role in a crisis. A mouse, for example, can be a comforting companion for a frightened child, offering a reassuring distraction in turbulent times. Even a small goldfish can calm the heart.

## CHOOSING SAFE LOCATIONS

When war or another crisis strikes, it's essential to be prepared for the worst. Finding or creating safe places is one of the most fundamental skills you can have in such situations. It's not just about finding a place to hide, but understanding what elements make a place safe and how to use your surroundings to your advantage.

### Understanding the Threats Around You

The first step is to understand the specific threat you're facing. In wartime, these might include bombing, gunfire, or invasion. In natural disasters, it could be floods, earthquakes, or fires. Each threat requires a particular type of protection. If you're in an area prone to bombing, look for locations that can shield you from shockwaves and fragments, such as basement rooms with thick concrete walls. For natural disasters like floods, seek higher ground and ensure access to clean water and food.

### Safe Locations in Nature

Nature can offer excellent hiding spots, but it requires knowledge of the terrain and natural dynamics. If you need to seek shelter outdoors, look for areas that are hard to detect. Dense forests provide natural camouflage and protection. Mountain areas can also be safe, especially if they have cliffs or caves that offer cover from the weather and aerial threats.

### Safe Locations in Urban Areas

In cities or built-up areas, finding safe spots might seem harder, but there are options if you know where to look. Basements are often good choices as they're below ground and can protect against explosions and gunfire. Thick concrete or brick walls are also essential. Avoid tall buildings, as they may collapse, and instead, look for low buildings with solid construction. Once, we had to take refuge in an abandoned factory in a war zone. Despite its age, it had thick concrete walls and an underground tunnel network, which provided both protection and a possible escape route if needed. We reinforced the doors with furniture and other materials we found, ensuring multiple exits for quick evacuation.

## Securing the Location

Once you've found a safe spot, it's crucial to make it even safer. This includes reinforcing entrances, creating camouflage, and setting up alert systems to detect enemies or other dangers. For example, you can set up simple tripwires using fishing line attached to small metal objects that make noise when stepped on, providing an early warning of anyone approaching. In one conflict area, we had to reinforce walls with sandbags and place furniture in front of windows to prevent fragments from entering if a bomb exploded nearby. We also used fabric and netting to camouflage the entrance, so it wouldn't be visible from the street. Additionally, we set up an escape route through another room leading to the backyard in case the main entrance was blocked.

## Access to Supplies

When securing a location, you also need to think about supplies. You'll need food, water, medicine, and protective equipment. If you plan to stay in one place for an extended period, ensure access to sanitation facilities or create an improvised setup. During prolonged crises, it may be necessary to forage or grow basic crops near your shelter. Once, in an isolated village under siege, we had to cultivate potatoes and vegetables in small patches we set up behind the house. We knew we'd be there for a while, and our food supply was running out. It was challenging to keep the crops hidden from the enemy, but it was essential for our survival. When on the move, carry seeds and plants suited to the area, and that grow quickly.

## BUILD MENTAL RESILIENCE

In addition to physical preparations, mental readiness is just as crucial. Knowing that you can make quick, accurate decisions under pressure could mean the difference between life and death. Always be prepared to relocate if the situation changes, and recognize that you may need to abandon a secured location if it becomes too dangerous to stay.

Over the years, I've learned that the ability to adapt quickly—both physically and mentally—is essential. The key is not to get locked into one strategy but to remain flexible and think several steps ahead. You must always be ready to act and not let fear take control.

Ultimately, creating or finding a safe place requires preparation and continuous assessment of the situation. Always be prepared to move if circumstances demand it. Remember, safety is not only about finding a physical location but also about being mentally prepared and ready to respond to the unexpected.

I hope that by applying these principles and experiences, you can prepare in a way that gives you the best chance to survive and protect those you care about.

# CHAPTER 3

# PROTECTION AGAINST PHYSICAL THREATS

In times of war or severe crises, physical threats can arise suddenly and unexpectedly. These may include direct violence from others or secondary threats such as fires or structural collapses. While most civilians do not have combat training, there are basic self-defense techniques that anyone can learn to protect themselves and their loved ones. This chapter focuses on how to handle such situations, both by preparing in advance and by taking appropriate action when threats arise.

## Basic Self-Defense Techniques

When law and order break down, you may find yourself facing dangerous situations where violence or threats to your life become a reality. Knowing basic self-defense techniques can give you a chance to protect yourself and your loved ones. It's not about becoming a fighter, but about being able to react quickly and effectively to avoid harm.

## Simple Techniques Anyone Can Learn

There are many simple self-defense techniques that can be learned in a short time, such as using everyday items for self-defense (for example, using a chair as a shield or a stick as a weapon). You should also learn how to protect vital areas of the body, such as the head and abdomen, and how to escape from an attacker. Even basic martial arts training can give you the skills needed to survive an assault.

## General Guidelines for Children

- Seek shelter if possible. Try to find a safe place, like a sturdy building or a room you can lock from the inside.

- Protect your head by using your hands and arms. If you have something to use as protection, like a jacket or backpack, hold it in front of your head.

- Curl up if you're on the ground or thrown down. Keep your arms over your head and face to minimize injuries.

- Keep your body tight and use your arms to protect vital areas, like your stomach and chest.

- Call for help if you can. Shout as loud as you can for assistance, or reach out to authorities or adults who can help.

- Avoid direct confrontation if possible. Find an escape route or create enough noise to attract attention so others can help.

## Basic Guidelines for Adults

- Stay calm; panic can lead to poor decisions. Try to keep a level head and assess the situation carefully.

- Seek shelter or escape if possible. Find a safe place to hide, like a building or a lockable room, or other forms of cover. If possible, try to get away as quickly as you can.

- Use your hands and arms to protect your head if you're attacked. If you have a bag or jacket, use it to shield your head.

- Keep your body tight and use your arms to protect vital areas, like your stomach and chest.

- If you must defend yourself physically, focus on blocking and escaping rather than striking back. Simple techniques, like using your elbows to protect your body or creating a barrier with your arms, can be helpful.

- Call for help by shouting or using your phone to contact emergency services. Provide a clear description of the situation and your location.

- If available, use resources that can serve as weapons. For example, an umbrella or other objects can help create distance or divert attention, allowing you to escape.

- The primary goal is to avoid confrontations and focus on protecting yourself and those with you.

## INTERACTING WITH STRANGERS DURING WAR

In a crisis, social trust can collapse, and people may become desperate. This can make strangers a potential threat, as they may try to take your supplies or harm you for their own gain. However, not all strangers are dangerous, and some might even become allies. In this section, I'll explain how to assess and handle such situations.

### Assessing a Stranger's Intentions

If you encounter strangers, whether on the road or near your home, it's crucial to quickly gauge their intentions. Look for signs of aggression, but also pay attention to body language and tone of voice. Desperation can sometimes lead to violence, even if that wasn't the initial intention. It's important not to show weakness, but also to avoid provocation. Don't reveal nervousness. Speak to strangers in a polite yet firm manner. Observe their body language and analyze their behavior without appearing as if you're assessing them.

Wondering how to read body language? Consider whether the person has an aggressive stance, a tone that makes you feel unsafe, or if they seem to have good intentions. Are they armed? Are there others nearby? Practice observing your surroundings and notice more than you would in a safe situation. Be discreet and decide carefully whether you'll trust the person. Never reveal to strangers what resources you have or how many people you're with. Your emergency supplies are for you and your family alone. Think safety in all that you do.

## Collaboration or Avoidance

In some cases, collaborating with strangers may be beneficial, especially if you share common goals, like survival. However, be cautious—collaboration should always happen on your terms, and you should have a plan to withdraw if the situation turns dangerous. If you decide to avoid contact, ensure you stay well hidden and move quietly to avoid detection.

# CHAPTER 4

# CARING FOR CHILDREN DURING CRISES

Children are especially vulnerable during war and crises, and it is our responsibility to protect and comfort them. This chapter focuses on how to ensure children's physical safety while also supporting their emotional and mental well-being. In a world filled with fear and uncertainty, children need stability and security—something that can only be achieved through deliberate efforts from adults.

## Why Children's Safety is a Priority

Children have a limited ability to understand and react to dangers, and they are more physically vulnerable than adults. This means their safety must be the highest priority in any crisis. Ensuring children's physical safety involves keeping them in a secure environment and having a plan to protect them from potential threats.

## How to Keep Children Safe in Various Situations

If you need to evacuate, make sure children are dressed appropriately for the weather and are always under supervision. Use simple systems like holding hands or using a leash to ensure that no one gets separated in chaotic situations. If you are in a shelter, set up a safe zone where children can be protected from hazards like sharp objects or open flames.

## Emotional Support and Security

Why emotional support is important? Children often respond to crises with fear and confusion. They may not fully understand what's happening but can sense the fear and stress in adults. Providing emotional support can help them cope with the situation, reducing long-term trauma and helping them feel secure, even in uncertain surroundings.

**Methods for Supporting Children Emotionally**

Use a calming tone when speaking to children and reassure them that you will protect them. Maintain routines as much as possible—such as regular mealtimes and bedtimes—to give them a sense of normalcy. Play can also be a valuable way for children to process what's happening around them. Let them draw, tell stories, or engage in role-play; it can help them express emotions they might otherwise struggle to articulate.

**How to Talk to Children**

When talking to children about war or other extreme situations where you may need to leave your home, it's essential to communicate with both empathy and clarity. Children need to understand what's happening without becoming overwhelmed with fear. Encourage them to be on your team to prevent creating more chaos than necessary. Share information in a way that is both informative and reassuring.

Use language appropriate to the child's age and understanding. Start the conversation in a calm tone and explain that sometimes things happen in the world that require quick decisions to stay safe. Reassure them that you are there to protect them and that, as a family, you will do everything possible to stay together and care for each other.

When explaining why you must leave home, use simple examples the child can relate to. For instance, compare the situation to evacuating during a fire drill at school or daycare. Explain that leaving home temporarily is a way to stay safe, just like leaving a building during a fire alarm. Be honest but avoid going into details that could be frightening.

If you have pets, it's important to be realistic but also comforting. Explain that in an emergency, you may not be able to take the pet immediately. Tell them that there are adults who work to help animals in these situations and that you will do your best to ensure the pet is also taken care of. This may include leaving food and water behind or informing animal protection services about the situation.

If the child is exposed to scenes of injured or deceased people, allow them the space to express their feelings. Explain that war and extreme situations can lead to people getting hurt and that many people are working hard to help those in need. Be available for questions and make sure the child knows it's entirely normal to feel scared or sad when witnessing something like this.

Give the child simple strategies to handle stress and fear, such as taking deep breaths, talking to a trusted adult, or drawing and writing about their feelings. Make it clear that talking about their emotions can be helpful.

Finally, remember that the child needs stability and hope. Tell them that although things may be difficult now, you will work together to get through it. Reassure them that, as a family, you are strong together and that you will do everything within your power to protect them.

This approach balances the need to provide essential information with the need to shield the child from overwhelming fear. You are their anchor right now, and they trust in you.

# CHAPTER 5

# MORAL AND ETHICAL DILEMMAS

In war or crises, people's basic morality and ethics can be challenged in ways they have never experienced before. When society breaks down and the usual rules of right and wrong become unclear, civilians may face difficult choices that go against values and principles. Under such conditions, desperate circumstances can force people to act in ways they would never have considered in a normal everyday situation. Understanding the potential moral and ethical dilemmas can help you prepare mentally and emotionally for the difficult decisions that may come.

This guide will highlight some of the most common dilemmas you might face. It will also give you an understanding of how to navigate these challenges while maintaining your humanity and ethical compass, even under extreme conditions.

### The need to protect yourself and others

One of the first dilemmas you may face in a crisis situation is balancing protecting yourself with helping others. In a chaotic situation where resources are limited and threats are many, it can be challenging to know how far to go to ensure your own safety and survival while considering the needs of others.

### Selfishness vs. altruism

In an emergency, you may face a choice of whether to share your resources with others or keep them for yourself and your loved ones.

This dilemma can feel even more acute when it involves resources such as food, water, or medicine, which can be crucial for survival.

**Scenario:** You have enough food to survive for a week, but you meet a family that has nothing. If you share with them, you risk your own supplies not lasting.

**Ethical assessment:** Should you help others at the expense of your own safety? Is it possible to find a middle ground where both parties can survive, or do you need to prioritize yourself and your loved ones?

### Protecting the Innocent vs. Protecting Yourself

Another dilemma arises when you witness violence and abuse against others. Should you attempt to intervene and protect the innocent, or withdraw to avoid putting your own safety at risk?

**Scenario:** You see someone being attacked or exploited in a situation where you have the chance to intervene, but doing so would put your own life in great danger.

**Ethical consideration:** Should you risk your own life to save others, or is it more prudent to withdraw and focus on protecting yourself and those you are responsible for?

## LOYALTY TO THE GROUP VS. LOYALTY TO HUMANITY

In war or crisis, loyalty to your own group – whether it's your family, community, or a survival group – can often come into conflict with broader ethical considerations regarding humanity. This tension can create deep moral dilemmas.

### In-group Loyalty vs. Justice

Situations may arise where our group makes decisions that you consider unethical. This could range from looting to exploiting weaker groups. You may be asked to support or participate in actions you would normally view as unjust or immoral.

**Scenario:** Your group decides to steal food from another vulnerable community to secure their own resources. This means that the group being looted could starve or suffer.

**Ethical consideration:** Should you follow the group's decisions to ensure your own survival, or should you stand against them and risk conflict or exclusion? Can you find a way that preserves both your moral values and the security of the group?

## CHOOSING ALLIANCES

In times of crisis, alliances may be necessary for survival, but this can involve working with individuals or groups that have different values from your own, or who engage in actions you cannot support.

Scenario: An armed militia offers protection in exchange for supplies from you or your group. This could secure safety in the short term, but it also means you are supporting a group that commits abuses against others.

Ethical consideration: Should you form an alliance to protect yourself, even though it means supporting injustice? How can you balance your survival instincts with ethical principles?

## LOOTING, THEFT, AND JUSTICE

When resources become scarce, many may be tempted to loot stores, homes, or other supply locations. This raises a fundamental question about property and justice in times of crisis.

### Stealing to Survive

Under normal circumstances, theft is illegal and unethical. But what if you steal to survive? What if you need to break into a store to access food or medicine that could save your life or someone else's?

**Scenario:** You have no food but see an unattended grocery store. Should you break in and take what you need to survive?

Ethical consideration: In such a situation, the question of necessity could be relevant. If resources are unavailable by other means, it may be ethically justifiable to take what you need to survive. But what happens when more people begin to think this way, and society gradually breaks down?

## PRESERVING JUSTICE

When law and order break down, civilians may be required to take responsibility for upholding some form of justice in their own communities. This may involve confronting those who are wronging others, even if it puts your own life at risk.

**Scenario:** A group of people is looting a local farmer who has managed to preserve some of their crops. You have no food yourself but understand that this will ruin the farmer's livelihood.

**Ethical consideration:** Should you attempt to defend the farmer's right to their property, even though this means going against the majority and putting yourself at risk?

## USE OF VIOLENCE AND SELF-DEFENSE

Violence in war or crises can often seem inevitable. Using violence to protect yourself or others may become necessary, but where should the line be drawn?

Self-defense is a natural response when faced with a threat, but crises can lead to situations where violence escalates unnecessarily. How can you balance the need for self-defense with the risk of causing harm to others?

**Scenario:** Someone tries to steal from you in a collapse scenario, and you have a weapon. You could use force to protect your belongings, but is it necessary to escalate it to deadly violence?

**Ethical consideration:** How can you best assess when violence is justified, and when there are alternatives that minimize harm? Where should the line for legitimate self-defense be drawn?

In a crisis or war situation, the world around you can transform in ways you never anticipated. When law and order break down, you may suddenly be faced with choices that challenge your basic moral and ethical values. As a civilian, without the formal training of military personnel or special forces, it can be difficult to navigate these situations while maintaining both your own survival and your humanity.

Through years of experience in extreme global crisis situations, I have seen the best and the worst in people. One thing that always strikes me is how humans, regardless of circumstances, have an exceptional ability to show humanity and morality, even when everything else is in chaos. Those who manage to preserve their inner strength, and who protect themselves while also caring for others, are the ones who look back on their actions with pride, no matter what the outcome of the situation may have been.

When you find yourself in a crisis, the pressure from external circumstances can be overwhelming. It is then, more than ever, that you must rely on the principles you have built up throughout your life. Moral clarity and preparation are key. It is always easier to make a decision when you have already reflected on potential dilemmas and determined what matters most to you. In an extreme situation, there is rarely time for long reflections. Therefore, it is crucial that you can act with a calm mind when it really counts. And this is why I don't provide answers to my scenarios and ethical considerations, so that you can reflect on what you would have chosen.

## PRESERVING HUMANITY UNDER PRESSURE

In situations where survival is at stake, your instincts may push you to act selfishly. However, experience shows that preserving your humanity in the face of inhumane conditions is crucial.

When this is over, you will look back on what you did. Were your actions aligned with your values? Can you live with the choices you made? These are questions you will one day have to ask yourself. Choosing humanity, as far as possible, makes it easier to bear the weight of what you went through when the crisis ends.

I have seen many people who, in desperation, chose the selfish path and later suffered more from their own actions than from the crisis itself. On the other hand, I have also witnessed countless examples of people sharing their last supplies, risking their own lives to protect others, and showing incredible compassion in the face of the horrors of war. They are remembered as individuals who gained something far more important than a fight for survival; they preserved their dignity and ethical compass.

## PRACTICAL CONSIDERATIONS AND WISDOM

While it is important to preserve your ethical integrity, it is also necessary to take practical considerations into account. Always evaluate the risks and consequences of your actions. In a crisis, you must be prepared to make difficult decisions, but these must be based on a balance between morality and necessity. Here are some practical pieces of advice to keep in mind:

**Prioritize safety, but be open to helping others.**

In many cases, helping others will strengthen your own chances of survival. Alliances and cooperation can be crucial in a crisis, and offering help can create bonds that last throughout the crisis. At the same time, you must set clear boundaries to safeguard the security of yourself and your loved ones.

**Mentally prepare for tough choices.**

Stealing to survive, having to leave someone behind, or using violence in self-defense are dilemmas no one wants to face, but they can become a reality in extreme situations. By mentally preparing for these possibilities now, you will be better equipped to make quick but thoughtful decisions when the time comes.

**Find a balance between loyalty and fairness.**

In some cases, your loyalty to your family, group, or community may come into conflict with what is fair on a larger scale. It is important to find a balance that ensures both the survival of your community and the preservation of your own moral integrity. Be honest with yourself: What actions can you live with, and which ones will be too difficult to carry with you afterward?

**Be aware of the dangers of violence.**

Violence may often seem like a simple solution in a pressured situation, but it tends to escalate quickly. Experience shows that those who avoid unnecessary violence often emerge with stronger mental health once the crisis is over. If you must use violence, make sure it is a last resort, and that you have considered all other alternatives first.

**One Final Piece of Advice**

No one knows how they will react in an extreme situation until they are actually in it. When you find yourself in a crisis, remember that it will eventually end. When that happens, you will look back on your actions. Make sure you can stand tall and know that you did your best.

It is often in the most extreme circumstances that people show their true selves. Let your true self be a reflection of your best qualities – strength, humanity, and wisdom. Survival is not just about living through the crisis, but also about living with the choices you make along the way. Be brave, be wise, and be human.

When the situation becomes too dangerous to stay, it may become necessary to flee. Being on the run is one of the most challenging situations a person can experience. You will rely on your ability to adapt to new environments quickly, handle unexpected threats, and secure the most basic needs such as food, water, and protection.

In this chapter, I will go through how you can prepare for fleeing, and how you can survive along the way.

*CHAPTER 6*

# ON THE RUN

**Packing for Fleeing – Why Preparation is Key to Survival**

A well-prepared escape plan can be the difference between life and death. When you are on the run, you cannot rely on finding what you need along the way. Therefore, it is crucial to pack an emergency bag with everything you need to survive for at least 72 hours. See chapter 1 for the emergency bag contents list.

**Survival While Fleeing**

Surviving while fleeing is a unique and complex challenge that differs from other forms of survival in several key ways. Here is a detailed review of why escape situations are especially demanding and the aspects that make them unique.

**Constant Changes in the Environment**

During flight, it is important to understand that the environment you operate in can change quickly and unexpectedly. You must constantly navigate through unfamiliar and potentially hostile areas. This requires constant assessment and adaptation to new conditions, whether it involves terrain, weather, or cultural norms.

**Ongoing Threats**

One of the most challenging aspects of fleeing is the persistent threat from enemies or pursuers. This threat can be physical, in the form of soldiers or armed groups, or psychological, as in cases of systematic surveillance and intelligence gathering. This means you must not only handle physical challenges but also remain constantly alert to psychological and strategic threats.

### Limited Access to Resources

When fleeing, you often have limited access to essential resources such as food, water, medical help, and shelter. This creates a continuous struggle to meet basic needs under time pressure. Efficient resource management becomes essential, and you must often improvise solutions based on the available resources.

### Social and Cultural Barriers

In many cases, you will be forced to navigate through areas with unfamiliar social and cultural norms. Understanding and adapting to these norms is crucial to avoid attention and to acquire necessary resources. Doing this without standing out requires significant strategic thinking and cultural sensitivity.

### Physical and Psychological Strain

Fleeing can be extremely physically and mentally demanding. Prolonged movement under difficult conditions, along with the constant fear of detection, can lead to exhaustion and stress. It is crucial to maintain physical health through constant assessment of your condition and effective stress management.

### Strategic Planning and Decision-Making

Effective flight requires detailed strategic planning and quick decision-making. Every movement must be carefully considered to minimize the risk of detection and maximize the chances of finding refuge or achieving safety. This also involves the ability to adapt to changing circumstances and act on short notice.

### Communication and Technology

During flight, it is often necessary to communicate securely and effectively with support personnel or allies. The use of technology to maintain communication and coordinate movements can be crucial, but you must also be cautious of technology's vulnerabilities and avoid surveillance.

## Long-Term Survival

Even if the immediate threat is over, there is often a need to secure long-term survival. This may involve finding a new and safe place to stay, building new alliances or networks, and restoring a normal life after fleeing.

Mastering survival while fleeing requires a combination of skills: resource management, cultural understanding, physical strength, psychological endurance, and strategic thinking.

## NAVIGATION WITHOUT MODERN TOOLS

In many situations, you won't be able to rely on GPS or other modern devices. Learn to use a map and compass, and understand how to navigate by the stars at night. Find landmarks like mountains, rivers, or roads, and use these to stay on course. If you lose your way, don't panic. Stop, take time to calm yourself, and assess the situation before proceeding.

### A Quick Reminder on How to Use a Map and Compass

Different maps have different scales. If the map reads 1:50,000, it means that 1 cm on the map represents 50,000 cm in reality. Divide by 100 to get the number of meters. Understand the type of map you have and orient yourself according to how the map's elements describe the topography in nature. Invest in a good map that can withstand water. At night, it's advantageous to use red light to read the map. It doesn't affect your night vision, and red light doesn't travel far.

Digital devices require power and resources, so being able to navigate with a map and compass will be a huge advantage when fleeing. It's important that everyone you're traveling with knows how to read a map and use a compass in case something happens. The map is usually oriented so that the top points north. The compass also shows the direction to north with the magnetic needle pointing to the magnetic north pole.

### How to Use a Map and Compass

- Hold the compass in front of you and orient the map so that the north on the map matches the needle pointing north on the compass.

- Keep mobile phones, metal, and iron away, as they can interfere with the compass needle.

- Decide on your destination and study the map to find the smartest route. Learn to read the topography on the map and consider the safest route. A straight line is not always the safest or fastest path. If the topography shows very steep terrain, it might be a difficult route. Also, consider the route based on who and what you have with you. If you need to climb or cross rivers, you might not be able to bring your companions with you.

- Once you've selected your route, move in that direction and check regularly that you're going the right way in relation to the map. Check as often as possible. Verify by looking at landmarks or the topography of the landscape.

### Tips for Finding Your Way Without a Map

If you're unfamiliar with the area, you'll need to use the landscape to track where you are at all times. Know where the sun rises and sets. This will help you identify where north, south, east, and west are. Follow riverbeds if you're in a forest or on a mountain, as rivers or streams will flow downhill, out towards water or the sea. Ant hills can also serve as good guides, as the main surface faces south. This is because ants seek as much sunlight as possible.

Look at the trees. The side where the branches are longest will be facing south. In winter, snow will melt faster on slopes facing south. If you're north of the equator and the sun is at its highest, it will be facing south. If you're south of the equator and the sun is at its highest, it will be facing north. These natural tips can serve as an emergency solution, but they don't always give the correct answer. However, remember that the sun always rises in the east and sets in the west.

## SLEEP AND REST – HOW TO MAINTAIN STRENGTH

Sleep and rest are critical components of any survival strategy, especially during a flight. While it may seem like a secondary priority in a situation characterized by immediate danger and stress, it is actually crucial for maintaining both physical and mental strength. Here's an in-depth review of why sleep and rest are so important in a flight situation, based on personal experiences.

### Physical Recovery

When the body is under continuous strain—whether from physical activity like moving quickly through terrain, carrying heavy gear, or from stress and exhaustion—it is essential that it has enough time to repair itself. Sleep and rest allow the muscles to recover, reduce muscle soreness, and repair tissue damage. Without sufficient rest, physical endurance will quickly decrease, impacting your ability to continue the flight effectively.

Stay warm by using leaves, clothes, or other available materials for insulation. Always stay alert to sounds or movements around you, and have a plan in place to get to safety if necessary.

### Mental Clarity and Decision-Making

Sleep deprivation negatively affects cognitive function, which can impair decision-making and strategic thinking. During a flight, being able to make quick and well-considered decisions is vital. Lack of sleep increases the risk of misjudgments and strategic errors that can be life-threatening. A rested brain is better equipped to handle stress, solve problems, and operate in complex situations.

### Body's Stress Responses

Sleep plays a key role in regulating the body's stress responses. Chronic sleep deprivation can lead to increased levels of stress hormones, such as cortisol, which can worsen both physical and psychological conditions. During a flight, an increase in stress hormones makes the situation even harder to handle. Regular sleep helps maintain a healthy balance.

## Immune System Function

Lack of sleep weakens the immune system, increasing vulnerability to diseases and infections. When on the run, it's important to minimize the risk of health problems that could hinder the ability to continue the flight. A strong immune system is crucial for handling the physical demands and dangers associated with a flight situation.

## Immunity Against Exhaustion

18 hours without sleep can produce symptoms similar to having a blood alcohol level of 0.5‰, and 24 hours without sleep can be equivalent to 1.0‰. Prolonged sleep deprivation leads to exhaustion, which in turn affects the ability to perform even simple tasks. Fatigue reduces reaction times and coordination and generally weakens physical capacity. On a flight, where efficiency and responsiveness are critical, even low levels of fatigue can have serious consequences.

## Mental State and Resilience

Adequate sleep helps maintain good mental health and emotional stability. During a flight, you might experience significant psychological stress, and a good night's sleep helps preserve mental resilience and the ability to cope with anxiety and fear. This is essential for maintaining focus and motivation during challenging times.

## Strategic Rest

Even in a flight situation, rest periods must be planned strategically. This involves identifying safe areas and times when you can get a brief but effective rest. Sleep needs must be adapted to the operational situation. Using available time and creating a safe environment for rest are crucial for balancing the need for rest with the necessary activity and mobility.

Sleep and rest are not a luxury in a flight situation, but an essential part of the survival strategy to maintain physical strength, mental clarity, and overall health. A thorough understanding of how and when to rest can be the difference between success and failure during a flight.

## FOOD AND WATER IN FLIGHT – HOW TO OBTAIN AND PRESERVE IT

In any survival situation, whether it's a natural disaster, war, or another emergency, securing access to food and water is the highest priority. Our bodies rely on a continuous supply of energy and fluid to maintain vital functions. Without food, the body starts breaking down fat and muscle mass to produce energy, which can eventually lead to organ failure. Without water, dehydration can occur in as little as 1–4 days, which can quickly become life-threatening.

To survive in a crisis, you must be prepared to act quickly and effectively. This requires a deep understanding of how to gather and preserve food and water, whether you're in an urban environment or out in the wilderness. Below, I'll discuss methods for obtaining resources, how to identify them, and techniques for ensuring these resources are safe to consume. Whether you're an experienced hunter, an urban survivalist, or someone who wants to be prepared, this information is crucial.

## METHODS FOR OBTAINING FOOD

### Foraging

Nature is full of edible plants, berries, mushrooms, and nuts, but it requires knowledge to know what's safe to eat. Foraging involves using what's naturally around you.

**Plants:** In Norway, plants like dandelion, nettles, and wild garlic are not only edible but also nutritious. Nettles can be boiled into a nutrient-rich soup, while dandelion leaves can be eaten raw or cooked.

**Berries:** Blueberries, lingonberries, and wild strawberries are safe choices. Avoid berries you can't identify with certainty, as some can be toxic.

**Mushrooms:** Foraging for mushrooms requires extra caution. Chantarelle and porcini are good options, but many other mushrooms are deadly. If you're unsure, it's better to leave the mushroom where it is.

**To succeed at foraging, you should:**

**Know the local species:** Learn to identify plants, berries, and mushrooms in your area. Become familiar with the most common poisonous plants like belladonna, hemlock, and wolf's bane. Knowing how to identify these can save your life.

**Avoid polluted areas:** Look for food in areas far from industrial sites and roads, where the soil may be contaminated.

**Test cautiously:** If you're unsure about a plant, do a skin test by rubbing a small amount on the inside of your elbow and wait for about 24 hours. If you don't have a reaction, try a tiny bit on your tongue and wait again. If there's no reaction, the plant is usually safe to eat.

## HUNTING AND FISHING

**Hunting:** If you have experience with hunting and the necessary equipment, this can be a vital way to obtain protein. Small game such as hare and birds, as well as larger prey like deer and elk, can provide significant amounts of meat. Always follow hunting laws and regulations, but be prepared to make decisions based on survival needs in an emergency.

**Traps:** Learn how to set simple snares or traps to catch small game. This can save energy compared to active hunting.

**Fishing:** Fish are an excellent source of both protein and essential fats. With a simple fishing rod or line, you can catch fish from lakes, rivers, or the sea. Use natural bait such as insects or small fish to increase your chances.

### Bartering and Trade

In situations where some form of social structure remains, bartering can be a viable strategy. Trade surplus items like clothes, tools, or medicine for food or water. Be cautious about revealing your resources, as this could attract unwanted attention.

## METHODS FOR OBTAINING WATER

### Natural Sources

**Rivers and Streams:** Freshwater sources like rivers, streams, and lakes are often the most reliable places to find water. However, even if the water looks clear, it may contain invisible dangers like bacteria, parasites, or chemical pollutants.

**Purification:** Boiling is the safest method to kill pathogens in water. If you don't have the means to boil water, a portable water filter or purification tablets may be necessary.

**Springs:** A spring is a natural water source from the ground. Spring water is often clean, but it's still advisable to filter or boil it to be safe.

### Rainwater Collection

Rainwater can be a valuable source of drinking water, especially in areas where it rains frequently. Use large surfaces like tarps or plastic sheets to collect rainwater. Pour the water into clean containers and let it sit for a while so the sediment can settle before boiling it.

### Dew and Condensation

In desert areas or other dry environments, you can collect water from dew or condensation. This is done by creating a solar still: dig a hole in the ground, place a container in the middle, cover the hole with plastic film, and put a stone in the center of the plastic. As the sun heats the ground, water will evaporate and condense on the plastic, dripping into the container.

By mastering these techniques and being aware of how to safely obtain and preserve food and water, you'll be better equipped to survive in an emergency situation. Whether you're in a rural or urban environment, securing these resources will be essential to maintaining your strength and health.

## STORAGE AND HANDLING OF FOOD

The quality and safety of food depend greatly on how it is stored. Proper storage can prevent food waste and protect against food-borne illnesses.

## Methods of Storage

**Drying:** Dry foods like fruits, vegetables, or meat to extend their shelf life. Use a dehydrator or sunlight.

**Cooking and Canning:** Cooking or canning techniques can also preserve food for longer periods. Be aware of the processes to ensure the food is not contaminated.

**Refrigeration and Freezing:** If you have access to electricity, use a refrigerator and freezer to store perishable foods. Make sure these appliances work under crisis conditions.

## Cooking Methods Without Electricity

**Cooking Devices:** Use a camping stove (primus) or a campfire when electricity is unavailable. Ensure you have enough fuel and a safe cooking space.

**Cold Food:** Prepare meals that do not require heating, such as pre-made salads or raw foods. This can be a simple solution in conditions with limited energy access.

## FOOD THAT TAKES UP TO 30 MINUTES TO PREPARE

Nut and Berry Mix

### Ingredients
Nuts: Hazelnuts, walnuts, or other edible nuts.
Berries: Blueberries, raspberries, lingonberries, or other edible berries.

### Instructions
- Gather the nuts and berries.
- Make sure you can recognize the edible varieties.
- Clean the nuts.
- Remove shells and any impurities.
- Mix together.
- Combine the nuts and berries in a container or a piece of cloth.

**Tip:** This mix provides both fast and slow carbohydrates, healthy fats, and proteins. It is easy to carry and requires no preparation.

Grilled Fish on a Skewer

**Ingredients**
Fresh fish: Caught from a river, lake, or the sea.
Skewer: A clean stick or branch.

**Instructions**
- Catch a fish using simple fishing techniques, such as a line, spear, or net.
- Clean the fish.
- Remove the innards and scales.
- Skewer the fish.
- Build a fire.
- Hold the fish over the flame, turning it regularly for 15–20 minutes until it is fully cooked.

**Tip:** Fish is an excellent source of protein and provides long-lasting energy. Make sure the fish is well-cooked to avoid food poisoning.

Wild Vegetable Soup

**Ingredients**
Edible plants: Nettle, dandelion leaves, wild onion, or other known edible plants.
Water: From a clean source.
Container: A metal can or heatproof container.

**Instructions**
- Gather the plants. Only pick those you are sure are edible.
- Clean the plants.
- Rinse them in clean, cold water.
- Build a fire.
- Boil water.
- Place the plants in the container and pour water over them.

- Cook over the fire and let the soup boil for 10–15 minutes until the plants are soft.

**Tip:** The soup provides important vitamins and minerals. Nettle is rich in iron and loses its stinging effect after boiling.

**Important to Remember**

**Identification:** Always be sure you can identify edible plants and animals. Avoid anything you are unsure of.

**Hygiene:** Wash your hands and food as thoroughly as possible to avoid illness.

**Fire:** Make sure to light the fire safely and extinguish it completely after use.

These recipes are designed to help you survive when resources are scarce. Stay hopeful, and remember that nature can be a valuable ally in difficult times.

# CHAPTER 7

# TRADE AND BARTER

In a crisis or war situation, traditional economic systems can collapse, and money quickly loses its value. When infrastructure breaks down, supply lines are cut, and law and order disappear, it may become necessary to revert to more primitive forms of economic exchange—trade and barter. For many civilians who have never been in a war situation, navigating this form of exchange can feel unfamiliar and overwhelming. However, understanding how to trade and barter in an effective and safe way can be crucial for survival.

## PRACTICAL TRADE AND BARTER DURING CRISIS AND WAR SITUATIONS

Through many years in crisis and war zones around the world, I have witnessed how people adapt in extreme situations. Some have survived by being skilled negotiators, while others have put themselves in danger due to poor preparation or a lack of understanding of the social dynamics of bartering. This guide aims to provide you with insight on how to engage in trade and barter in a safe, effective, and morally responsible manner.

### Understanding the Value of Goods in a Crisis Situation

When society is in a crisis, the value of goods will change dramatically from what you are used to in a normal economy. Goods that were previously easily available may suddenly become extremely valuable, while things like jewelry, money, or luxury items may lose all their value.

## Essential Goods Become the New Currency

In times of crisis, food, water, medicine, and fuel will become some of the most valuable trade goods. These are things that people cannot live without, and therefore they will have high barter value. For example:

- Food and water will cost anything if people are starving. Dry goods like rice, pasta, canned food, and water purification tablets will have very high value. A kilo of rice in a desperate situation could be more valuable than gold jewelry.

- Medicines, antibiotics, painkillers, and even simple bandages can save lives and therefore have high value.

- Fuel and light sources. In situations where electricity is unavailable, fuel, candles, lighters, and batteries will become extremely valuable.

## Goods That Lose Value

Money: When the economy collapses, cash quickly loses its value. If there are no stores to shop at or functioning banks, money becomes worthless.

Luxury Goods: Jewelry, electronics, designer clothes, and other luxury items will not have the same value in a crisis, as these items do not contribute to survival.

## Plan the Barter Carefully

Entering into a barter situation without a plan can be risky, both for your own safety and for the outcome of the trade. Here are some important tips on how to plan and prepare before engaging in barter.

## Understand What You Have to Offer

The first thing you should do is make a list of the things you have that might be valuable to others. This could include food, water, clothing, tools, medicines, or other supplies. Carefully consider what you can spare without putting yourself at risk. For example:

Food: If you have a stock of dry goods, you might consider trading a small portion of it to acquire other necessities, like medicine or tools. But be careful—since food is often the most valuable resource, it should only be traded when you're certain you have enough for yourself.

Tools and Equipment: Simple things like flashlights, knives, or ropes can be invaluable in a crisis. If you have duplicates or excess of these items, they can be very useful in barter.

## Get an Overview of What You Need

Before entering a barter situation, you must have a clear understanding of what you need. It may be tempting to trade for anything, but focus on the things that will be most useful for your survival. Remember: Don't trade away anything you can't replace if you truly need it later.

## Find the Right Trade Partner

During times of crisis, many will be looking to barter goods. However, it's important to be selective when choosing who to trade with. Try to barter with people you trust, such as family, friends, or community members. Trading with strangers can be risky, especially if they are desperate or violent.

## Tactical Execution of the Barter

Once you've identified what you want to trade and who you want to trade with, it's important to execute the transaction in a safe and effective manner.

## Negotiate Wisely

Bartering requires negotiation skills. When trading goods, always be mindful that the other party might try to take advantage of the situation. Here are some negotiation tips:

- **Stay Calm and Firm:** Show that you know the value of what you're trading away. If you seem desperate, the other party may try to push you into a worse deal.

- **Be Flexible:** If the other party doesn't have what you originally wanted to trade for, be open to other offers that might meet your needs. Maybe they can offer services, like repairing equipment, that could also be valuable.

- **Be Aware of Getting Scammed:** In some cases, it may be hard to know if the goods you're receiving are authentic or of good quality. For example, medicines might be counterfeit or expired. Learn how to inspect goods carefully before finalizing the trade.

## Safety During the Trade

Bartering can sometimes be risky, especially when resources are scarce and desperation is high. Here are some important safety tips:

- **Avoid Revealing All Your Resources:** If people know you have large amounts of food or valuable goods, you could become a target for theft or violence. Only show what you're intending to trade, and avoid displaying your entire stockpile.

- **Choose a Safe Location for the Trade:** Avoid trading in places where it's easy to get ambushed. Choose an open, neutral space with good visibility. If possible, bring along one or more reliable people to ensure the trade goes smoothly.

- **Be Prepared for the Deal to Go Wrong:** Even if you take all precautions, things can still go awry. Have a plan for what to do if the trade escalates into threats or violence.

## Ethical Considerations in Bartering

Even in times of crisis, it's important to maintain a certain degree of morality and ethics in barter. This is especially important for maintaining good relationships with the community and other survivors. People are social beings, and crises have shown that those who cooperate and maintain a certain level of fairness tend to have a greater chance of long-term survival.

## Don't Exploit Others' Misfortune

Even if you have something valuable and could demand a lot for it, it's important to remember that we're all in the same situation during a crisis. Exploiting others' desperation can lead to resentment and long-term conflicts. Show compassion by offering fair barter deals that benefit both parties.

## Build Trust

By demonstrating honesty and reliability in your bartering, you can build trust in the community. Trust can be as valuable as the goods you're trading, as people will be more willing to trade with you again in the future if they know you're fair.

## One Last Tip

Bartering is more than just a transaction; it's a complex, human interaction that requires planning, tactics, morality, and a deep understanding of your surroundings. By preparing yourself both mentally and practically now, you can be ready to face the challenges that may arise. Not only will you secure your own supplies, but you will also build trust and relationships, and perhaps even create a small community that shares the values of fairness and survival.

Remember that in times of crisis, it's not just the goods you're trading that have value—the value also lies in how you trade and the relationships you build. Trading with wisdom, ethics, and careful strategy is not only the path to survival but also the way to preserve your integrity and humanity in the face of the most extreme conditions.

# CHAPTER 8

# WHEN WAR OR CRISIS ERUPT

When war breaks out or a crisis strikes, the world suddenly and brutally changes. For most civilians, this is the moment when life is turned upside down. Normal routines and the safety of everyday life are replaced by uncertainty, fear, and often a fight for survival. In such circumstances, we are reminded of how fragile our lives really are and how quickly we can lose the most basic rights that we take for granted.

## My Experiences

For my part, I have witnessed how war and crises affect ordinary people—people like you and me—in ways that can be difficult to imagine until you're in the midst of it. Homes are destroyed, families are torn apart, and what was once safe communities are transformed into chaotic zones where survival is the only thing that matters.

Civilians have certain rights during times of war and crisis, rights intended to protect them from the worst atrocities that war and crises bring. These rights are enshrined in various international treaties and conventions, such as the Geneva Conventions, which are designed to protect those not involved in the fighting—meaning ordinary civilians, medical personnel, aid workers, and others. The Geneva Conventions, for example, state that civilians should not be the target of military attacks, and they should be protected from violence, humiliation, and discrimination. However, in practice, there is often a significant gap between what is written on paper and what actually happens on the ground.

During the Balkan War in the 1990s, a conflict I was partially involved in through my role, we saw how civilians were targeted through ethnic cleansing, mass rapes, and other war crimes—even though these actions were clear violations of international law. Such examples illustrate how fragile these rights can be when war rages, and how dependent civilians are on the international community to actually enforce the laws.

In crisis situations that do not involve armed conflict but still threaten people's lives and well-being—such as natural disasters or pandemics—civilians also have the right to protection and assistance. These rights are also enshrined in international documents, such as the UN Declaration of Human Rights and various treaties on humanitarian aid. Here, we have seen mixed follow-up, with some countries quickly mobilizing to protect their citizens, while others fail or choose not to do the same. During the earthquake in Haiti in 2010, many were left without access to necessary aid for a long time, despite being entitled to it. This caused massive unrest and major riots, damaging people and property.

When we talk about the likelihood of civilian rights being upheld during war and crises, we must sadly acknowledge that it often depends on several factors, including the intensity of the conflict, the type of government or authorities involved, and the degree to which the international community intervenes. Often, civilian rights are set aside in the most desperate situations, where survival is the top priority, and the laws meant to protect them are broken with no fear of consequences.

Nevertheless, it is important to remember that these rights exist for a reason—they are an expression of the global community's agreement that, even in the darkest times, there is a minimum of human dignity and respect that must be upheld. As civilians, we can find strength in knowing that there are laws meant to protect us, and we can encourage our leaders and the international community to enforce them.

For many who live in peaceful and stable societies, it can be difficult to imagine the reality during war or crisis. But we must not forget that we all, no matter where we live, can be affected by such events. Therefore, it is crucial that we understand what rights we have, how we can prepare, and what we can expect from those appointed to protect us. Through knowledge and preparation, we can be better equipped to face the unexpected and support each other through critical times.

## EVERYDAY LIFE IN WAR AND CRISIS

When war or crisis strikes, daily life transforms dramatically. It is no longer marked by ordinary tasks like work, school, and leisure, but by a constant fight for survival. Every day brings new challenges, and both physical and mental strength are required to get through them.

The most basic needs—such as food, water, and safety—often become the biggest challenges. In several of the conflicts I've been involved in, access to clean water and enough food has been a luxury many had to do without. I've seen families forced to leave their homes, their lives reduced to what they can carry on their backs. Refugee camps often become a refuge for many, but even these are far from safe havens. Overcrowding, poor sanitary conditions, and lack of resources make life in these camps a daily struggle.

But extreme crises like natural disasters and war are not just about physical threats and strain. The mental burden can be even more devastating than the physical one. Anxiety, depression, and post-traumatic stress disorder (PTSD) are common companions in these situations. I particularly remember an event during a Middle Eastern conflict where a mother I met had lost all her children in a single day due to a bombing raid. The grief and desperation she radiated is something I will never forget. Mental health is often overlooked in war and crises, but it is one of the most important factors for survival and the ability to rebuild life afterward.

## Rights Under Pressure

In theory, civilians are protected by a number of international conventions and treaties during war and crises. The Geneva Conventions, as mentioned earlier, are a central document that defines how warring parties should treat civilians. Civilians should not be targets of military attacks, they should be protected from violence and humiliation, and they should have the right to assistance if they are injured or sick. But in practice, we often see these rights being ignored, especially in conflicts where the state has collapsed or where non-state actors like militia groups dominate.

One example that illustrates this is the civil war in Syria, where civilians have been targeted on a large scale through the use of chemical weapons, siege tactics that starve entire cities, and indiscriminate airstrikes on residential areas. Despite such actions being clear violations of international law, the international community has struggled to protect civilians and enforce these laws. This shows how difficult it can be to ensure that the rights of civilians are upheld, especially in complex and protracted conflicts.

However, there are also examples where the international community has managed to uphold civilian rights. In the Kosovo War in the late 1990s, NATO intervened to protect civilians from ethnic cleansing. Although military intervention is always controversial, it ultimately provided some degree of protection for the civilian population.

## What Civilians Can Do

Although many of the factors influencing a civilian's situation in war and crisis are beyond their control, there are still measures that can be taken to increase the chances of protection and survival. First and foremost, it's important to be prepared. Having an emergency plan, including an escape route, stored supplies, and knowledge of where to seek help, can make a significant difference. I have seen examples of communities that have set up their own alert systems and support networks to protect each other when the authorities have failed.

For others, it's crucial to know their rights and seek support from international organizations like the Red Cross, the UN, or volunteer organizations. These organizations can provide emergency aid, medical treatment, and legal support. In the conflict situations I have been in, these organizations have been the only hope for many..

# CHAPTER 9

# COMMUNICATION AND INFORMATION

In a crisis or war situation, information becomes one of the most valuable resources you can have. Information can help you make decisions that save lives, protect yourself and your loved ones, and ensure access to necessary resources. However, misinformation and rumors can spread like wildfire, especially in times of uncertainty. In these situations, it's crucial to know how to differentiate between credible information and rumors that may put you in danger or lead to poor decisions.

For several years, I have operated in some of the world's most unstable areas, where information has been both a lifeline and a threat. In situations where law and order have broken down, I've witnessed how rumors and fake news have led to panic, violence, and chaos. This guide will provide insight into how you, as a civilian, can navigate the often chaotic and confusing landscape of information, and provide concrete strategies for how to verify and use information wisely.

## HOW TO DIFFERENTIATE BETWEEN RELIABLE INFORMATION AND RUMORS

When a crisis occurs, news sources you normally trust may become unavailable or influenced by the unfolding events. This can create a vacuum often filled by rumors, speculation, and disinformation. Understanding how to distinguish between reliable information and rumors is the first and most important step in a crisis situation.

### Source Criticism

In a crisis situation, it's essential to assess the source of the information you receive. Before acting on any information, ask yourself:

- Where does the information come from? Is it from an official source, such as a public statement or a well-known and trusted news organization, or from an informal source, like a friend or acquaintance who "heard something"?

- Is the source known for accuracy? If the information comes from a person or source that has previously provided reliable information, you can give it more weight than if it comes from someone known for spreading rumors or exaggerations.

- Is the information confirmed by multiple independent sources? In a crisis, it's important to see if multiple credible sources are reporting the same thing. If a piece of information comes from just one source, and no one else is reporting the same, you should be skeptical.

## Assess the Credibility of the Content

Too good or too bad to be true? Extreme claims—whether they announce a miraculous solution or an impending disaster—are often suspicious. Be especially cautious with information that plays on fear or hope in an extreme way.
Does it lack details or specifics? Be skeptical of information that lacks concrete details. General statements like "everyone is fleeing now" or "everything is destroyed" can be exaggerations if they can't be backed up with specific facts.

## How to Handle Rumors

Rumors spread particularly quickly in times of crisis because people are uncertain and scared, desperately seeking answers. Rumors can spread through all forms of communication, including social media, phone calls, or face-to-face conversations. The problem with rumors is that they are often based on incomplete or distorted facts and can lead to dangerous actions.

## Never Spread a Rumor Until It's Confirmed

Even though it may be tempting to share information you've heard in an effort to help others, spreading rumors can create panic and chaos. Before sharing information, do your best to confirm it from multiple sources. If you can't confirm it, it's safest not to share it at all.

## Assess the Intention Behind the Rumors

In war and crises, there are often actors who intentionally spread disinformation to gain an advantage, whether they are military forces, criminal groups, or others with their own agendas. For example, fake messages about evacuation routes may be used to lure people into dangerous situations. Always ask yourself: Who benefits from me believing this rumor?

## Be Cautious with Social Media

Social media can be a significant source of disinformation in crisis situations. Many posts and news may seem credible but are entirely false. If you use social media to stay updated, make sure the information is from official accounts or verified sources. Images and videos can be manipulated, and what appears to be a real event might be misleading or taken out of context.

## HOW TO VERIFY INFORMATION

In a situation where credible information may be hard to come by, it's essential to develop the skill to verify information on your own. Cross-check information from multiple sources:

## Direct Observation

If possible, try to observe the situation with your own eyes. For example, if rumors are circulating about a particular road being dangerous, you might try to confirm this by speaking to people who have recently traveled that route or by checking from a safe distance.

## Use Technology to Your Advantage

If you have access to the internet or other communication tools, use services that provide reliable real-time information. Many international organizations like the UN and the Red Cross, as well as trusted news organizations, will often have real-time updates on the situation.

## How to Use Information to Make Decisions

Once you've verified the information, it's important to use it strategically to make the right decisions. Information is only valuable if it leads to actions that improve your situation.

## Use Information to Plan

**Evacuation and Safety:** If you receive reliable information about a safe evacuation route or a secure area, use the information to plan how you and your loved ones can get there. Double-check the route and make sure you have alternative plans in case the situation changes.

**Resource Management:** If you hear about potential food supplies or safe water sources, assess whether the information is reliable and if it's worth the risk to travel there.

## Adapt Quickly to Changes

The situation in a war or crisis can change rapidly, and what was safe today may be dangerous tomorrow. Make sure you continuously update yourself with reliable information, and adapt your plans accordingly. Flexibility is key to survival.

## Communication with Others

When you have reliable information, share it with your loved ones or trusted individuals. Keeping the community informed with accurate information can save lives and reduce panic.


## HOW TO HANDLE DISINFORMATION AND PSYCHOLOGICAL WARFARE

In wartime and crisis situations, disinformation is often part of a deliberate strategy by opposing parties to confuse, demoralize, or weaken their adversaries. This is known as psychological warfare. It can involve spreading fake news, manipulating facts, or planting rumors to create panic, distrust, or misguided decisions. Understanding that you might be a target of such tactics is essential to avoid being manipulated into making poor choices.

## Identify Signs of Disinformation

Targeted Misinformation: In war situations, parties may intentionally spread rumors about, for example, upcoming attacks or evacuations to destabilize opponents or create chaos among civilians. If a message appears designed to instill fear or chaos without providing specific details, it may be a sign of disinformation. Excessive Optimism or Pessimism: Both extremes — messages claiming "everything is under control" or "total catastrophe" — can be strategically planted to influence reactions. In such cases, always seek confirmation from independent sources.

## Stay Calm in the Face of Psychological Warfare

Psychological warfare is designed to break down your willpower and create uncertainty. It's important not to act impulsively based on emotions like fear or anger when you hear rumors or see information that may seem alarming.

- **Remain Rational:** Always ask yourself, "What is this information trying to get me to do?" If the answer is that you feel pressured to act quickly and without thinking, it's a warning sign. Step back and critically assess the information.

- **Verify Everything, Especially Critical Information:** If a message or rumor seems too good or too bad to be true, put in extra effort to verify the information. Use multiple, reliable sources, especially when the information comes from unknown or unofficial channels.

- **Consult Trusted People or Sources:** In many cases, community leaders, aid organizations, or local authorities may have more reliable information. Make sure to double-check critical details with these sources before taking action.

## Secure Your Communication Systems

It's crucial to understand that in a crisis, your communication could be monitored or intercepted by hostile parties, including national authorities, terrorist groups, criminals, or others looking to exploit the situation.

## WHY COMMUNICATION SECURITY IS NECESSARY

Secure communication protects against information failures and prevents data misuse. This is especially important in a crisis when your safety may be at risk. In emergencies, misinformation or adversaries intercepting your communication can lead to significant losses, both human and material. If the opposing side knows your plans or whereabouts, they can easily manipulate or attack you. Therefore, all communication should be as secure as possible.

## Methods for Securing Communication

- **Encryption:** All electronic communication should be encrypted, especially if using messaging apps or email. Encrypted services like Signal or ProtonMail provide extra layers of protection and make it extremely difficult for unauthorized parties to read your messages. Use encrypted communication tools for sending sensitive messages. Many modern apps offer end-to-end encryption to protect the content of your communications.

- **Switch Channels Frequently:** Don't use the same communication channel for too long. Change channels often but not necessarily at the same intervals. Also, switch to different tools and methods to make it harder for hostile actors to track you or adapt to your routines.

- **Use One-Time Codes and Numbers:** If you need to send especially sensitive messages, consider using one-time codes or numbers that only the recipient knows. This way, only those with the correct code can interpret the message.

- **Avoid Sharing Too Much Information:** Even when communicating securely, it's wise to avoid sharing too much information. Remember that the less others know, the harder it is for them to use it against you.

- **Password Protection:** Ensure that your devices are password-protected to prevent unauthorized access to your personal data.

- **Redundant Systems:** Have multiple communication channels available, such as radio, phone, and emergency markers, to ensure you can stay informed even if one method fails.

## BUILDING AN INFORMATION NETWORK

In a crisis, it can be helpful to establish a local information network with trusted individuals. This can provide a secure way to share and verify information and protect against rumors and disinformation.

### Sources of Reliable Information

Having access to information is not enough; you also need to assess whether it is reliable. In crises, false rumors, disinformation, and propaganda often abound. To determine if a source is trustworthy, ask yourself the following questions:

- Where does the information come from? Is it from an official source, an eyewitness account, or a rumor? Official government sources are generally more reliable than unofficial ones.
- Is the information verified? Can you find the same information from multiple, independent sources? If so, it is likely to be more reliable.
- Is the information consistent? If the information you receive is contradictory or very different from other trustworthy sources, be skeptical.

### Three Key Tips

1. Public Warning Systems: Pay attention to alerts and recommendations from local authorities. They often provide essential information about evacuations, protective measures, and safety procedures.
2. Health Organizations: Stay updated with advice from health organizations like WHO or local health authorities on health risks and protective measures.
3. Local Networks: Collaborate with neighbors and the local community to share information and resources. This can be a helpful way to get updates and support.

### Communication Methods

Selecting the right communication tools during crises is crucial. Depending on availability and circumstances, some methods may be more appropriate than others. Below are several communication methods, each with its own advantages and disadvantages:

### Verbal Communication

Face-to-face communication is the most fundamental method and, in many cases, the safest if you can control your surroundings. However, it requires physical contact, and parts of the message can be lost due to human error. Additionally, information can be intercepted or compromised if you need to travel through unsafe areas. This method is time-consuming and poses risks, especially if intercepted by adversaries.

### Mobile Phones and Radio Communication

Mobile phones are the most common communication tool today, but they may be unreliable in crisis situations. Networks might be down or intentionally disabled, and signals can be tracked. Hand-held VHF or UHF radios can be more reliable, especially in areas where mobile networks are unavailable. However, radio signals can also be intercepted by hostile actors.

### Emergency Signs and Signaling

Simple methods like emergency flags, smoke signals, light flashes, mirrors, flags, or whistles can be critical when other methods fail. While these may seem primitive, they are highly effective when technology is unavailable or has collapsed.

## Digital Messaging Systems

Encrypted messaging platforms such as Signal or Telegram may offer more security than standard messaging apps. However, they are not immune to surveillance, particularly if adversaries have sophisticated resources.

## Satellite Phones

Satellite phones can be invaluable when mobile networks are down, as they communicate directly with satellites without relying on ground networks. However, they can be expensive and challenging to operate.

## Analog Radio

Shortwave or CB radios are good alternatives in areas with poor infrastructure. These are also used by emergency services and can be critical in emergencies.

## Paper Maps and Compass

While not a communication tool per se, having access to paper maps and a compass is essential for navigation. Digital maps may fail if power or network access is unavailable.

## Radio

Battery-operated or solar-powered radios can provide access to news and emergency alerts. Tune into local stations for updates.

## Inform the Right People

Once you have verified information that could be life-saving, share it with those who need it, such as neighbors, community leaders, or aid organizations. Be selective, especially if you are uncertain about someone's intentions or loyalty.

### When Information is Unavailable

One of the most challenging situations during a crisis is the absence of reliable information. Lack of information can lead to decisions driven by fear or uncertainty.

### Prepare for Information Shortages

Ensure you have alternative ways to access information, such as a battery-powered or emergency radio. These can be invaluable when conventional channels like the internet or mobile networks fail. Familiarize yourself with official alert systems in your area and have the necessary tools, such as a radio tuned to emergency frequencies.

## MAKE DELIBERATE CHOICES IN THE ABSENCE OF INFORMATION

When information is scarce, it's easy to become paralyzed or make poor decisions. In such cases, rely on your preparations and make decisions based on what you know. If you must act without reliable information, proceed cautiously and avoid unnecessary risks.

### Learn from Past Crises

Looking at lessons from past wars and crises can provide valuable insights into what works and what doesn't. During the 2004 tsunami in Southeast Asia, a massive international relief effort was mobilized quickly. Many lives were saved due to the swift response, but others suffered unnecessarily due to bureaucracy and a lack of local knowledge among international responders. This highlights the importance of both national and international preparedness and the need for aid to be tailored to local conditions.

While no one wishes to face war or crisis, for many, it becomes an unavoidable reality. Civilians cannot always prevent what lies ahead, but they can prepare as best as possible, know their rights, and seek support from the international community. Through collaboration, knowledge, and solidarity, we can increase our chances of survival and contribute to rebuilding once the crisis subsides.

# CHAPTER 10

# MEDICAL CARE AND FIRST AID

In crisis situations, access to medical assistance may be limited or completely unavailable. Therefore, it is crucial to have basic knowledge of first aid and medical care. This chapter provides a practical guide on how to handle medical emergencies, both for yourself and others, and how to prepare for such challenges.

In an emergency, every minute counts. Proper first aid can prevent infections, reduce pain, and even save lives before professional medical help arrives. Having a well-equipped first aid kit and knowing how to use it is essential.

**A well-equipped first aid kit should include:**

- **Bandages and plasters:** To cover wounds and prevent infection.

- **Antiseptics:** Such as alcohol or iodine solution to clean wounds.

- **Painkillers:** Like ibuprofen or paracetamol to manage pain and fever.

- **Medical gloves:** To protect both you and others while treating wounds.

- **Scissors and tweezers:** For cutting bandages and removing foreign objects.

### Basic First Aid Techniques

- **Cardiopulmonary Resuscitation (CPR):** If someone is unconscious and not breathing, start CPR with 30 chest compressions followed by two rescue breaths.

- **Stopping bleeding:** Apply pressure to stop bleeding from large wounds. Place bandages over the wound and press firmly. If bleeding doesn't stop, apply a tourniquet above the wound.

- **Treating burns:** Cool the burn with lukewarm water for at least 20 minutes and cover it with a sterile, non-stick bandage. Avoid using ice directly on the burn.

### Managing Specific Injuries

Different types of injuries require different treatment methods. Knowing how to handle specific injuries can improve the chances of successful recovery and prevent complications.

### Common Injuries and Treatments:

- **Fractures and sprains:** Stabilize the fracture with an improvised splint and avoid moving the injured area. For sprains, use the R.I.C.E. method (Rest, Ice, Compression, Elevation).

- **Poisoning:** If poisoning is suspected, try to identify what was ingested and seek help immediately. Do not drink water or induce vomiting without consulting a medical professional.

- **Eye injuries:** Rinse the eye gently with clean water or saline solution for at least 15 minutes. Avoid rubbing the eye, and seek medical help as soon as possible.

### Managing Psychological Stress

Psychological stress can be as serious as physical injuries in a crisis situation. Stress, anxiety, and trauma can affect your ability to handle the situation effectively. It is important to address mental health, both in yourself and those around you.

**Methods for Managing Stress:**

- **Breathing techniques:** Deep breathing can reduce anxiety and help you stay calm. Try breathing in through your nose for 4 seconds, holding your breath for 4 seconds, and exhaling through your mouth for 6 seconds.

- **Support and communication:** Talk to others who are experiencing similar challenges. Sharing thoughts and feelings can reduce stress and foster a sense of community.

- **Physical activity:** Light exercise or walking can help lower stress hormones and improve your mood.

By preparing both physically and mentally, you can enhance your ability to handle medical emergencies and the challenges of a crisis effectively.

# CHAPTER 11

# LEGAL AND SOCIAL ASPECTS OF CRISES

In a crisis or war situation, civilians are often the most vulnerable, caught between warring factions and destroyed infrastructure. Even when it feels like law and order are breaking down, it is essential to understand that civilians still have protected rights under international law. These rights are upheld through various treaties, conventions, and international agreements designed to safeguard people during war and crises. Knowing these rights can provide you with reassurance and guidance during a time when justice and safety may seem out of reach.

Through many years of experience in crisis management worldwide, I have witnessed how international law operates in practice, both when it is respected and when it is violated. Below, I explain the rights you have, the laws and conventions that apply, and who is responsible for enforcing these protections.

**International Laws and Agreements Protecting Civilians**

In both war and crisis situations, several international agreements and laws are in place to ensure that civilians are treated with dignity and respect. Some of the most important include:

**The Geneva Conventions (1949)**

The Geneva Conventions are the cornerstone of international humanitarian law, aimed at protecting those who are not participating in the fighting, including civilians. These conventions apply in both international and internal conflicts and cover four main areas:

- **Protection of the wounded and sick:** Civilians who are

injured or ill during a conflict must be treated with respect and provided with necessary medical care, regardless of their affiliation.

- **Protection of shipwrecked soldiers:** While primarily addressing military personnel, this principle highlights the importance of safeguarding anyone unable to participate in combat, including civilians caught in the conflict.

- **Treatment of prisoners of war:** Although this mainly pertains to military personnel, civilians captured during a conflict are also considered protected.

- **Protection of civilians during wartime:** This is especially critical, as it prohibits attacks on civilians, including bombings and other direct violence against non-combatants.

The Geneva Conventions also forbid collective punishment, hostage-taking, and the use of starvation as a tactic of war. These actions are considered war crimes, and individuals who commit such acts can be held accountable under international law.

## Additional Protocols to the Geneva Conventions (1977)

These protocols expand the protection of civilians during modern conflicts, including internal conflicts (civil wars). They emphasize the prohibition of attacks on civilians and civilian property, requiring warring parties to distinguish between military targets and civilians.

## Key Points from the Protocols:

- **Prohibition of direct attacks on civilians:** Warfare must be limited to military objectives. Civilians should not be subjected to direct attacks, and infrastructure such as water supplies and healthcare services must be protected.

- **Prohibition of indiscriminate attacks:** Attacks that fail to clearly distinguish between military and civilian targets, or that cause unnecessary suffering to civilians, are prohibited.

## The UN Universal Declaration of Human Rights (1948)

Although not specifically designed for war situations, this declaration establishes fundamental rights that remain applicable during war and crises. Key rights include the right to life, liberty, and personal security, as well as access to adequate living conditions, including food, water, housing, and healthcare.

## Important Provisions:

No discrimination: The right to protection applies to everyone, regardless of nationality, ethnicity, gender, religion, or political affiliation.

## The Rome Statute of the International Criminal Court (1998, ICC)

The Rome Statute establishes the ICC's authority to investigate and prosecute individuals for crimes against humanity, war crimes, and genocide. The court can hold individuals, including military leaders and heads of state, accountable for serious violations of international humanitarian law.

Civilians can report war crimes to the ICC, and if the court has jurisdiction, it may investigate and prosecute those responsible.

## Implications of These Laws and Agreements for Civilians

These international laws and conventions have significant implications for you as a civilian during a crisis or war. The most important point to remember is that you have the right to protection, and no one should target you or other civilians in acts of warfare.

## 1. Protection from Attacks

As a civilian, you are protected under the Geneva Conventions from being targeted in military operations. This means warring parties have a legal obligation to avoid civilian casualties and harm as much as possible. You also have the right to remain in your home unless evacuation is necessary for your safety. Forced displacement of civilians is illegal except in rare cases where it is in their best interest, such as evacuation from a conflict zone.

## 2. Access to Essential Resources

You are entitled to access basic necessities, including food, water, and medical aid. In conflict zones, warring parties have a legal obligation to allow humanitarian organizations to provide access to these resources.

Using starvation as a weapon is prohibited under international law. Civilians cannot be denied food supplies as a means of forcing surrender or agreement.

## 3. Right to Humanitarian Aid

You have the right to receive humanitarian assistance from organizations such as the UN, Red Cross, and other international aid groups. Warring parties are required to allow humanitarian actors to deliver aid to those in need, and deliberately blocking or obstructing such efforts is unlawful.

## 4. Right to Humane Treatment

If captured or otherwise interacting with hostile forces, you are entitled to be treated with dignity and respect. This includes protection from torture, degrading treatment, or punishment, and ensuring your basic needs are met while in their custody.

## WHO IS RESPONSIBLE FOR UPHOLDING THESE RIGHTS?

### 1. State Authorities and Military Leaders

Governments and military leaders bear the primary responsibility for protecting civilians. This includes ensuring that their forces comply with international regulations. Failure to do so can result in accountability for war crimes.

### 2. The International Criminal Court (ICC)

The ICC investigates and prosecutes individuals, including political and military leaders, for war crimes, crimes against humanity, and genocide. Reports of violations of the Geneva Conventions or other international laws can prompt investigations by the ICC.

### 3. International Organizations

The UN and Red Cross play vital roles in protecting civilians during crises and conflicts. They monitor adherence to international humanitarian law, report violations, and provide humanitarian aid.

The Red Cross, in particular, is recognized under the Geneva Conventions as a neutral party, granted access to conflict zones to protect and assist civilians and monitor the treatment of prisoners of war.

The UN High Commissioner for Human Rights (OHCHR) is another key actor, monitoring human rights abuses during crises and ensuring compliance with international standards.

### 4. Local Authorities and Actors

While international laws exist, local authorities and leaders are often responsible for ensuring civilians are protected and humanitarian aid is delivered. This includes government representatives, community leaders, or humanitarian organizations operating on the ground.

### 5. Media and Civil Society

Media play a critical role in documenting and reporting violations of international laws. By highlighting war crimes or civilian mistreatment, media outlets contribute to holding perpetrators accountable and creating global pressure to uphold legal standards.

Civil society organizations, both national and international, also contribute by documenting human rights violations and advocating for justice for those affected.

## WHAT CAN YOU DO IF YOUR RIGHTS ARE VIOLATED?

Even with robust international laws and agreements, there may be situations where your rights as a civilian are violated during a crisis or war. If this occurs, several actions can be taken to seek protection or justice:

### 1. Document Incidents

If it is safe and possible, try to document any abuses or violations of your rights. This may include taking photos or videos or recording witness statements. Such evidence can be crucial if you later report the incident to international authorities like the Red Cross or the UN.

## 2. Seek Help from Humanitarian Organizations

Reach out to international aid organizations like the UN or the Red Cross, which can assist with humanitarian relief and advocate for your rights. These organizations are mandated to help civilians suffering during wars and crises and can escalate your case.

## 3. Report War Crimes

If you witness or are a victim of war crimes, you can report these to relevant international bodies such as the ICC or human rights organizations. Although the legal process may take time, these reports help ensure accountability for perpetrators.

## 4. Protect Yourself and Your Family

In situations where your rights are systematically violated, such as in cases of violence or forced displacement, focus on safeguarding yourself and your loved ones. This might involve finding a safe location, seeking refuge in camps, or working with humanitarian organizations for evacuation.

In times of chaos, understanding your legal rights can equip you with the tools needed to protect yourself, seek justice, and navigate the dangerous situations that arise. Even in the darkest times, laws and agreements exist to uphold human dignity and hold those responsible for abuses and war crimes accountable.

## LEGAL RIGHTS AND RESPONSIBILITIES

Understanding your legal rights and responsibilities can shield you from abuse and help you navigate the legal system during crises. This includes issues related to property, contracts, and rights associated with emergency assistance.

### Addressing Legal Issues

- Property and Ownership: Ensure you have documentation of ownership, and be aware of how the crisis may impact your rights.

- Contracts and Agreements: Review contracts to understand your obligations and rights. In some cases, renegotiation or exceptions may be necessary due to the crisis.

- Seek Assistance: If you face legal challenges, reach out to volunteer organizations or legal advisors for support and guidance.

## BUILDING AND MAINTAINING COMMUNITY

When war or crises occur, society is often torn apart at all levels – socially, economically, and politically. For civilians who suddenly find themselves in a world where normal societal structures have collapsed, the ability to interact with others in a constructive way can be crucial for survival and later rebuilding.

In such a time, social interaction – the ability to collaborate and share resources – will be essential for creating a sustainable community.

**Here are examples of actions you can take:**

- Voluntary Work: Participate in or organize volunteer activities to help your community. This can include repairs, educational programs, or support for those in need.

- Joint Projects: Work with others to create joint projects that can strengthen the structure of the community, such as starting local initiatives or events.

- Communication and Collaboration: Maintain open communication with neighbors and local communities to share information and resources, and support each other.

**Solidarity and Social Interaction During Crises**

Based on my long experience in conflict situations worldwide, I would like to share some insights on how we humans can navigate through these extremely challenging situations. Although crises and wars tend to bring out the worst in some, history shows us that they can also bring out the best in humanity – solidarity, cooperation, and compassion. To rebuild a community after such an event requires not only physical reconstruction but also a deep understanding of social, cultural, religious, and geographical differences that may influence how people interact with each other. This guide aims to provide advice to civilians worldwide, regardless of background, on how to navigate socially in times of crisis and contribute to rebuilding afterward.

In a crisis or war situation where society's traditional structures such as the police, authorities, and social services break down, a vacuum emerges where people and local communities must take responsibility for creating safety, organizing, and sharing resources. Building trust, interacting with others in a respectful manner, and ensuring that everyone in the community is heard and respected are crucial for survival.

**Create Small but Strong Communities**

The first step in any crisis situation is to find people you can trust, who can help ensure basic needs such as food, water, and safety. Small communities, where each member has a clear role, often have a greater chance of surviving and thriving in the chaos that follows a crisis.

- **Divide Tasks and Responsibilities:** In crises, organizing labor becomes crucial. Divide tasks based on people's skills. Some may have medical experience, others may know the local geography or have technical skills. By leveraging people's strengths, you can build a robust network that can withstand the pressure of the crisis.

- **Build Trust and Communication:** Trust is the glue that holds a community together during times of crisis. Even in situations where you do not know all the members of your community, it is important to communicate openly and honestly. Discussions about resources, security, and future plans must be transparent to avoid distrust and internal division.

- **Hold Regular Meetings:** Set regular times to meet and discuss challenges. Giving everyone a voice in the decision-making process, regardless of background or status, builds a sense of community and common goals.

- **Share Resources:** In times of crisis, resources such as food, water, medicine, and shelter can be very limited. Instead of everyone trying to secure themselves, cooperation is the key to survival. By sharing resources fairly, you ensure that no one in the community is left without the basics they need to survive.

- **Resource Sharing Etiquette:** Develop a simple but fair way of distributing resources. Ensure that the most vulnerable, such as children, the elderly, and the sick, are prioritized. This will not only strengthen the community's bonds but also ensure that the community as a whole has a better chance of survival.

## HANDLING DIFFERENCES IN CULTURE, RELIGION, ETHNICITY, AND GEOGRAPHY

In any crisis, differences between people will be highlighted, whether they are cultural, religious, ethnic, or geographical. Such differences can lead to divisions, but they can also be a source of strength if handled correctly. Understanding and respecting these differences is essential for building an inclusive community both during and after a crisis.

- **Cultural and Religious Sensitivity:** Crises can lead to stress and fear, which often amplify differences between people. To prevent these differences from causing conflict, it is important to be sensitive to others' beliefs and traditions.

- **Respect Different Rituals and Practices:** In communities where people have different religious or cultural backgrounds, it is important to make space for each other's practices, especially during difficult times. Some may need to pray at specific times, while others may follow particular dietary rules. Respect for such differences helps bridge gaps between people.

## ETHNIC AND GEOGRAPHICAL DIFFERENCES

In crisis situations, old tensions between ethnic groups can flare up, especially if resources are scarce. It is important to actively work on building bridges between different ethnic groups. This can be done by focusing on common interests and goals, such as survival and safety.

- **Geographical Differences and Knowledge:** People from different geographical areas may have varying experiences with surviving in different terrain or climate conditions. Sharing this knowledge is valuable for adapting to the situation, whether you are in a desert area, a tropical jungle, or an urban environment.

- **Common Rules for Handling Conflict:** In any situation where different people are gathered, conflicts may arise. This is especially true in high-stress situations such as war or natural disasters. Therefore, it is important to have clear guidelines for how conflicts should be handled before they escalate into violence.

- **Dialogue and Mediation:** When conflicts arise, the community should have a process for dialogue and mediation, where neutral parties help find solutions. This could involve local leaders, elders, or respected community members who have the trust of both sides.

# CHAPTER 12

## REBUILDING

When the war or crisis is finally over, the real challenge begins: rebuilding. This is not just a process of repairing broken buildings or infrastructure, but also a time when we must piece our lives back together, both personally and as a community.

Through many years of active crisis management around the world, I have witnessed countless crises and conflicts up close. Each situation is unique, but common to them all is that the road back to normalcy is never easy. This is where our true courage is tested – not in the fight itself, but in the ability to rise again afterward.

I have personally witnessed communities that have been shattered, but I have also seen the incredible human spirit that refuses to be broken. People who, despite loss and destruction, find the strength to start anew. Rebuilding is about more than bricks and mortar; it requires time, patience, and a deep understanding of what has been lost and what is needed to restore hope, strengthen our communities, and ensure that we stand stronger together than we did before the crisis.

In this chapter, I will share insights and experiences on how we can contribute to rebuilding, not just as individuals but as part of a larger community. This is about you, your home, your community – about how we can all play a role in building a better future together. Through practical advice and personal reflections, I hope to provide you with the tools you need to navigate this difficult but essential phase after the crisis.

## RE-ESTABLISHING COMMUNITIES

After a crisis, the strength of the community is crucial for rebuilding. It is in the community that we find support, resources, and the collective forces needed to rebuild what has been destroyed. Working together with neighbors, friends, and local leaders creates a stronger platform for collective effort.

Start by participating in local initiatives aimed at rebuilding, whether it's cleaning up the area, repairing schools and healthcare institutions, or participating in the planning of new infrastructure projects. Be an active participant in organizing volunteer work, creating new support groups, and offering help to the most vulnerable. Remember, rebuilding social bonds is just as important as rebuilding physical structures.

After a crisis, people need something to hold onto, something that reminds them that life can move forward. Restoring normal daily routines and activities can be a powerful form of healing. This includes everything from reopening schools and shops to organizing community activities like sports or cultural events.

Start by establishing routines in daily life. This can be as simple as having regular meals, getting back to work, or sending the children back to school. While not everything will be as it was before, routines provide a sense of stability. It is also important to find new ways to adapt to the reality you live in now. This could involve learning new skills, finding new jobs, or developing new ways to achieve what was once part of everyday life.

## PLANNING FOR FUTURE RESILIENCE

After experiencing a crisis, it is important to learn from the experiences and build a stronger, more resilient future. Resilience is about being able to withstand and recover from future crises, whether they are similar or entirely different in nature.

Start by creating a long-term plan that takes into account potential threats in the future. This may include improving infrastructure, building more robust housing, and developing better emergency protocols. Invest in education and training that provides the community with the tools they need to handle crises more effectively next time. Create a culture of preparedness where everyone is involved in keeping the community safe and informed.

## RECOVERY OF PERSONAL FINANCES

A stable economy provides the foundation for maintaining a good quality of life and rebuilding a future after a crisis. Having a plan for financial recovery can help you manage debt, secure necessary funds, and rebuild financial resources.

### Strategies for Financial Recovery

- **Budgeting:** Create a realistic budget plan that takes into account your income and expenses. Prioritize necessary expenses like food, shelter, and medical care.

- **Securing Income:** Look for opportunities for temporary or long-term income sources, whether through work, voluntary contributions, or support programs.

- **Debt Management:** Contact creditors to negotiate payment plans or installment agreements to manage debt that has arisen as a result of the crisis.

## RESOURCE MANAGEMENT

Effective resource management is key to ensuring that you can meet your needs sustainably. Proper handling of resources can reduce waste, maximize utility, and contribute to long-term stability.

### Methods for Resource Management

- Planning and Distribution: Make a plan for how to use your resources efficiently. Prioritize the most essential resources and ensure they are fairly distributed.

- **Inventory Management:** Keep track of what you have in stock and use it before it expires. Implement a system to monitor resource usage and avoid unnecessary waste.

- **Recycling and Reusing:** Find ways to recycle and reuse materials to reduce the need for new resources. This may also include repairing equipment or swapping goods with others.

## LEADERSHIP AND REPRESENTATION

During recovery, there is often a need for leaders who can organize efforts and represent the community to authorities and aid organizations. These leaders should be selected based on their ability to listen, understand, and act on behalf of everyone in the community, not just based on personal interests.

### Leader's Responsibilities

A leader in a community under reconstruction must primarily focus on promoting cooperation, sharing resources fairly, and ensuring that the community takes collective responsibility for its own future.

### Economic Reconstruction and Cooperation

A crucial part of post-crisis community building is restoring the local economy. This may begin on a small scale, with people sharing services, skills, and resources, and grow into more formal economic structures as the community stabilizes. Economic cooperation is essential, especially in areas where resources are scarce, and external aid may be limited or unavailable.

- **Barter and Collective Effort:** In crisis situations, or when a community is trying to rise after a disaster, barter can be an effective way to distribute resources. If money no longer holds the same value, food, medicine, labor, and skills can be exchanged for other necessities. This is especially important in communities with limited access to external resources.

- **Community Work and Effort:** For the community to thrive again, people must be willing to contribute to the collective rebuilding effort – such as repairing schools, water supplies, and housing. Cooperation across social divides is essential for everyone to benefit from the effort and to avoid divisions based on economic or social status.

## RECOVERY OF SOCIAL SERVICES AND EDUCATION

Another key factor in reconstruction is ensuring that the community's basic social services are restored. Schools, healthcare services, and other infrastructure that can help the community return to normal function must be prioritized early in the process.

- **Education as the Key to the Future:** After a crisis, especially in conflict areas, children and youth may have missed valuable education. Restoring schools and educational services will not only help young people get back on track but also give them hope for the future. Education can also play an important role in building bridges between groups that have been in conflict by focusing on shared values and rebuilding.

- **Healthcare Services:** After crises, especially in communities with few resources, diseases and health problems can worsen. Building up local healthcare services, including access to medicines, clean water, and sanitation facilities, is crucial for the community to stand on its own again.

### Cultural and Religious Differences in Community Building

When a community is being rebuilt after a crisis or war, cultural and religious differences can either be a source of conflict or a strength that can contribute to mutual understanding and cooperation. It is essential to understand how to navigate these differences to ensure a harmonious society.

### Valuing Cultural Differences

Many communities are culturally diverse, which can be a challenge when trying to build a unified society after a crisis. But instead of viewing this diversity as a barrier, it should be seen as a resource. Different cultural practices can offer the community various ways to solve problems, whether it's about resource management, conflict resolution, or cooperation.

- **Cultural Celebration and Integration:** It's important to find ways to celebrate and include all cultural traditions in the new community. This can be done by organizing joint cultural celebrations, marking important holidays for different groups, and ensuring that everyone has the opportunity to express their cultural identity.

## RELIGIOUS UNDERSTANDING AND UNITY

Religion plays a central role in many people's lives, especially in times of crisis when people seek comfort and direction in their faith. It is important to make space for religious differences in the rebuilding process and ensure that religious leaders and institutions are included as part of the social fabric.

**Cooperation Among Religious Leaders:** One strategy that has proven effective in many crisis areas is for religious leaders from different faiths to come together to promote peace and cooperation. These leaders often have great influence in their communities, and their support for a community-focused rebuilding project can help bridge divides between groups that may otherwise be in conflict.

### Understanding Local Geography and Ethnic Divisions

Geographic and ethnic divides can often be accentuated in crisis situations. People from different regions or ethnic groups may have different interests or needs, especially when it comes to access to resources or political power. By understanding these differences and working actively to ensure a fair distribution of resources and power, divisions and conflicts in the new community can be prevented.

Geographic Diversity as a Strength: Different geographical areas may have different natural resources, such as food or water sources. Creating fair barter exchanges between these areas can strengthen the community as a whole and contribute to a more balanced reconstruction.

## LONG-TERM COMMUNITY BUILDING AND PREVENTION OF FUTURE CRISES

Even after a crisis has been resolved and the community begins to stabilize, it is important to continue building robust social structures that can prevent future crises. This includes both physical infrastructure and social systems designed to withstand future challenges.

### Creation of Permanent Institutions

After crises, the community must work to build permanent institutions that can provide stability and support for its members. This includes local governments, schools, healthcare services, and legal systems. By building strong and transparent institutions, the community will be better able to withstand future challenges.

**Social Safety Nets:** It is important to have social safety nets to help the most vulnerable members of the community, such as the elderly, sick, and children. This can include community funds, food banks, or other local arrangements to ensure that no one is left behind in the future.

## TRAINING AND COMPETENCE BUILDING

Communities that have been devastated by crisis must invest in training and competence building to stand on their own in the future. This can include training in practical skills like farming, construction, or medicine, but also in leadership and conflict resolution.

**Training Future Leaders:** Identifying and training future leaders who can represent the community's interests in the future is crucial. These leaders must have an understanding of the community's social, economic, and cultural needs, and they must be willing to put the community's needs above their own.

### Prevention of Future Conflicts

Conflict prevention is a key part of community building. The community must learn to identify sources of conflict before they escalate. This can include everything from political reforms to more direct conflict resolution mechanisms.

**Focus on Equality and Justice:** By ensuring that everyone in the community feels heard and valued, future conflicts can be prevented. This includes ensuring fair distribution of resources and access to power structures, so that no one feels marginalized or oppressed.

Community building does not require large economic resources alone, but rather a collective effort based on trust, cooperation, and sharing skills and resources. Even in the poorest communities, people have managed to build strong, resilient communities by focusing on what they have in common, rather than what divides them. No matter where you are on the planet, or what situation you are facing, there are always ways to work together to create a better and more sustainable society.

In the end, rebuilding is about more than just repairing buildings and infrastructure. It's about repairing social bonds, restoring trust, and ensuring that everyone in the community feels included and valued. Unity, sharing, and respect for differences are the keys to building a community that can withstand future challenges and give everyone a chance to thrive.

## The Future After the Crisis

Crises test human resources, but they also offer opportunities for growth and rebuilding. Once you've navigated the challenges and begin rebuilding, it's important to have a vision for the future. Work toward a sustainable, stable future with strength and compassion. This book has provided you with the tools to survive and recover from crises. Now it's up to you to use them, create new opportunities, and shape a world where we can all thrive.